WOMEN: Looking Beyond 2000

D1228108

WOMEN: Looking Beyond 2000

 United Nations, New York, 1995

95-684

The views expressed in this book by Bella Abzug, Margaret Gallagher, Ama Ata Aidoo, Anita Anand, Martha Alter Chen, Mahbub ul Haq and Gertrude Mongella in the respective chapters are those of the authors and not necessarily those of the United Nations.

UNITED NATIONS PUBLICATIONS

United Nations, Room DC2-853, New York, New York 10017 USA

UNITED NATIONS PUBLICATIONS

Palais des Nations, 1211 Geneva 10, Switzerland

U.N. Sales No. E.95.I.40

ISBN 92-1-100592-2

Photo credits:

John Isaac/UN: Pp. 10, 17, 22, 40, 48, 78, 84, 85, 86, 104, 106, 120, 125

Ruth Massey/UNDP: P. iii

Maggie Murray-Lee/UNICEF: Pp. viii-ix

Charton/UNICEF: P. 2

Lemoyne/UNICEF: P. 32

Doranne Jacobson/UN: Pp. 38-39

Ray Witlin/UNDP: Pp. 48

Ray Witlin/UNICEF: P. 54

Peter Larsen/ UNICEF: P. 70

Carolyn Watson/UNICEF: P. 82

Betty Press/UNICEF: P. 92

Maggie Murray-Lee/UNICEF: Pp. 118-119

Design by Georgiana Goodwin

CONTENTS

PREFACE

This book is a successor to *WOMEN: Challenges to the Year* 2000. The latter volume was published in 1991 following the first review and appraisal of the Nairobi Forward-looking Strategies for the Advancement of Women to the Year 2000. The Forward-looking Strategies had been adopted at the conclusion of the third world conference on women, held in Nairobi, Kenya in 1985. *WOMEN: Challenges to the Year* 2000 was published as part of a worldwide educational campaign to increase awareness of the obstacles encountered in implementing the Nairobi Forward-looking Strategies.

Publication of this volume coincides with the Fourth World Conference on Women (Beijing, China, September 1995). Preparations for the Beijing Conference included a second review and appraisal of the Forward-looking Strategies. Once again, challenges and obstacles were uncovered. A Draft Platform for Action was approved, providing the main document for discussion and negotiation by Governments at Beijing.

The Platform for Action cites critical areas of concern to women and identifies obstacles to women's advancement in each critical area. *WOMEN: Looking Beyond* 2000 is published to help raise awareness of these obstacles and of actions to be taken to support women in attaining their rights and their full potential. The book includes up-to-date information about many of the critical areas of concern described in the Platform for Action. It concludes with a powerful call to action by Gertrude Mongella, Secretary-General of the Fourth World Conference on Women.

WOMEN: Looking Beyond 2000 was prepared by the United Nations Department of Public Information with the cooperation of other agencies and offices of the United Nations system.

HEALTH AND EDUCATION

REPRODUCTIVE HEALTH AND WOMEN'S RIGHTS

Women in most societies have many roles, but their role in reproduction is often the only one recognized, and even in that they can expect little support.

Most women must struggle to reconcile activities outside the home with their traditional roles. They cannot participate fully in economic and public life, have limited access to positions of influence and power, and have narrower occupational choices and lower earnings than men. Too often, they have little or no voice in decisions made inside or outside the household; too often even their reproductive health is neglected.

Enabling couples and individuals to choose when to have children and freeing women from the health risks associated with reproduction and sexuality are essential to redress these inequities, fulfil women's human rights and make it possible for countries to progress towards sustainable development, including the early stabilization of population.

This understanding is central to the landmark agreement reached by 180 nations at the International Conference on Population and Development (ICPD) in Cairo last September. The Programme of Action adopted by the Conference calls for gender equality and equity, for allowing women to have and exercise choices and for making reproductive health care available throughout the world.

The Programme of Action places human rights and well-being explicitly at the centre of all activities to achieve sustainable development. Rather than emphasizing human numbers and demographic targets, it stresses the well-being of individual women and men, and the need to invest in their health and education and in building equity and equality between the sexes.

The ability to exercise choice in regard to fertility has a strong impact on women's reproductive health and allows them to participate in social, political and economic activities. Making family planning available also reduces maternal morbidity and mortality, and helps to prevent the transmission of reproductive tract infections, sexually transmitted diseases and HIV/AIDS.

Improving women's status depends in the first instance on their personal autonomy, especially in the area of sexuality and reproduction. This means they must have access to reliable information, to quality family planning services and to the other services necessary for full reproductive health. Enabling women to make free and informed decisions about the number and spacing of their children is a key step in empowering them to exercise other choices and in acknowledging their many roles other than reproduction.

Experience around the world has shown that to address people's reproductive and sexual health needs, family planning services need to be integrated into a wider framework which addresses their overall health and well-being. Comprehensive reproductive health care can be built on the foundation of family planning programmes already existing in some 155 countries' primary health care systems, generally combining family planning with maternal and child health care.

Women's ability to improve their reproductive health also depends on their ability to make decisions in other aspects of their lives, and to participate fully in the life of the community. In addition to enhanced health services, improving women's health requires better living conditions and stronger roles in decision-making at all levels.

Together with health care, education is the most important intervention to break the vicious cycle of low status, poverty and large families. There is a direct connection between education for girls and women's ability to escape from poverty; education also encourages later marriage and greater use of contraception. It is associated with lower maternal mortality, with smaller, healthier families and with better reproductive health for the next generation.

Another important step is to encourage men to take responsibility for their sexual and reproductive behaviour and household obligations, to allow women to become equal partners in public and private life.

A comprehensive approach to reproductive health

Sefernesh, from Ethiopia, was given in marriage at age 10, and was pregnant at 13. She returned to her mother's house to give birth, where she suffered six days of agonizing labour. On the seventh day her husband finally sought medical assistance from the town's private clinic. The health assistant delivered her dead child; Sefernesh was left with an obstetric fistula, a serious reproductive health complication.

Mary, a mother of three from a small town near Delhi, India, suffered from vaginal infections for several years. When she finally saw a doctor, she was diagnosed as having gonorrhoea. The doctor gave her antibiotics and suggested she send her husband in for a treatment. The husband was furious, and refused to see the doctor. As a result, the infections came back and Mary continues to suffer.

While health issues related to reproduction and sexuality affect women and men of all ages, women bear most of the associated burden of ill health. Essential aspects of reproductive health include family planning, safe motherhood and prevention and treatment of reproductive tract infections and sexually transmitted diseases. A central achievement of the ICPD was its promotion of a comprehensive approach to meeting the totality of people's reproductive health needs, particularly those of women and girls.

To promote reproductive rights, the ICPD Programme of Action calls on all countries to provide universal access by 2015 or sooner to a full range of high-quality reproductive health services—including safe, effective, affordable and acceptable methods of family planning—through their primary health care systems.

Lack of information or opportunity prevents many women from using existing family planning services. In many countries, women need their husbands' consent for contraception or sterilization. Eliminating these obstacles would remove a serious threat to women's lives and health.

Even with limited resources, reproductive health programmes can provide information, education and counselling on sexually transmitted diseases and HIV/AIDS, and on barrier methods of contraception. Others may additionally offer pregnancy testing, pregnancy and infertility counselling, and prevention and management of reproductive tract infections and some sexually transmitted diseases, such as syphilis. Where infrastructure, staff and funding are sufficient, programmes may provide still wider services, including information for the prevention of abortion and management of abortion complications, post-partum maternal care and breast-feeding advice, HIV/AIDS prevention and counselling, and screening and outpatient care for other reproductive health conditions.

Care for women of all ages

The Women's Health Care Foundation (WHCF) in the Philippines offers comprehensive reproductive and other health care to all women throughout their life cycle, rather than focusing more narrowly, as most maternal and child health and family planning clinics do, on reproductive-age married women who are pregnant or have young children.

WHCF operates three Manila clinics, open six days a week. They offer obstetrics and gynaecological consultations and care, including family planning; management of reproductive tract infections, including sexually transmitted diseases; laboratory tests; counselling; and referral.

Each client is treated with respect and privacy — regardless of her ability to pay, motive, profession, social and marital status, age or health condition. Every client's complete medical history is taken, followed by a thorough physical examination. An efficient patient flow minimizes the time clients spend in the clinic; throughout their stay, clients are made to feel at ease. Those unable to pay in full may receive discounts or pay by instalment.

Each clinic has a medical officer, a nurse or midwife and a medical technician. All staff members are women, trained to advance WHCF's goals and philosophy. Ongoing staff training is conducted locally and abroad. All activities are regularly evaluated to improve policies and procedures.

After operating a clinic-based programme for several years, the staff realized they needed to reach women where they lived and worked. In 1991, with support from the United Nations Population Fund, WHCF set up a new clinic and an attached outreach programme. In poor communities, field staff conduct focus-group discussions and seminars with women and adolescent girls and boys.

For the future, WHCF plans to place more emphasis on information and communication for women, especially in reproductive health, and to expand its research and outreach programmes.

In the effort to expand health and family planning services in poor areas, attention has generally been focused on issues of quantity, accessibility and distribution of services. In recent years, however, it has become apparent that the quality and acceptability of care provided are also crucially important and deserve increased attention. This recognition has given rise to new indicators of quality.

Critical to how women experience services and whether they continue with medical care are the exchange of information between provider and client and the quality of interpersonal relations, provider competence and mechanisms to encourage follow-up visits. Also crucial are programme quality standards which are acceptable and achievable in the country's specific conditions. Information efforts are needed to increase women's knowledge about contraceptives and where to obtain them, and to address their concerns about health and side-effects associated with contraceptive use.

Special target groups: men and adolescents

Men play a major role in reproductive health and family planning, particularly in decisions about contraceptive use. But they have been largely invisible as a target group in family planning programmes, contributing to low levels of contraceptive prevalence and wasting the potential offered by primarily "male methods" of contraception. Reproductive health care programmes can take several steps to increase male involvement, including education, encouraging better communication between partners, making services more "male-friendly" and promoting community-based distribution of condoms.

In much of the world, young women have traditionally married and started bearing children at an early age. While this is still true for many, young women today are marrying later than in the past, in part because they stay in school longer. As the interval between the onset of sexual maturity and marriage increases, so does their exposure to the consequences of high-risk sexual relations—unwanted pregnancy, HIV/AIDS and other sexually transmitted diseases.

Married or not, very young women face much higher risks in pregnancy and childbirth than those who delay child-bearing until after age 20. They are less likely to continue their education and are more likely to have lower-paying jobs or to be jobless. They have a higher rate of separation and divorce. The ICPD Programme advocates education and counselling to promote responsible sexual behaviour and protect adolescents from unwanted pregnancies and sexually transmitted diseases. It also has services which recognize their needs, taking parents' responsibilities into account.

Migration to cities, deteriorating economic conditions and other lifestyle-changing factors are undermining traditional customs and family ties that have discouraged pre-marital sex. Providing sex education in schools can help protect teenagers from the risks of sexual activity. Various innovative means are also being used to reach out-of-school youth. Young people need access to counselling on family planning, gender relations, violence, prevention of sexually transmitted diseases, including HIV/AIDS, and prevention and treatment of sexual abuse and incest. In addition, they need access to reproductive health services including family planning, unrestricted by care providers' attitudes or legal and social barriers.

Some excellent programmes offering services for adolescents have been developed. In Jamaica, for example, a programme supported by the United Nations Population Fund operates women's centres in seven cities to help young mothers cope with the consequences of early pregnancy. Day care is provided to allow the women to continue their education. The centres also provide counselling, family life education and contraceptive services. Young fathers are encouraged to get involved in the programme, and many attend the weekly community workshops.

Elements of reproductive health care programmes

In developing countries, one third of the illnesses among women aged 15-44 are related to pregnancy, childbirth, abortion, HIV/AIDS and reproductive tract infections. High levels of maternal mortality and poor maternal health are closely related to the low social and economic status of women. Preventing unwanted pregnancy or protecting themselves against disease is difficult or even impossible for many women. Certain traditional practices compound women's poor health status.

Taking a broad approach to reproductive health care

A programme in Tunisia's Sfax maternity hospital integrates post-partum care, family planning and infant care. By tradition, a Tunisian mother exclusively cares for her newborn and abstains from sexual relations for 40 days after childbirth. On the fortieth day, a new mother in Sfax is encouraged to bring her baby to a health centre, where both are examined and the infant is immunized. At that time, a health worker discusses with the woman the importance of breast-feeding and gives her information about family planning and contraception. In 1987, 83 per cent of post-partum women in the city came to the clinic; 56 per cent of those women adopted a method of family planning, a high rate of success for a post-partum project.

The Brazilian Government, in cooperation with the women's movement, in 1983 initiated the Comprehensive Programme for Women's Health Care. Going beyond existing maternal and child services, the programme strives to empower women by offering a broad array of services and information which address reproductive health but also mental and occupational health. It serves women of all ages, from adolescents to post-menopausal women.

Costa Rica in 1989 established an integrated health programme. It includes services for maternal and child health, early detection of cervical and breast cancer, monitoring of pregnant women and women who have just given birth, and family planning. Another decree the same year created a National Council of Women's and Family Health to facilitate the implementation of maternal and child health policies and to formulate and put into effect a national health plan for mothers and newborns.

Safe motherhood: Three fourths of maternal deaths worldwide can be attributed to haemorrhage, infection, pregnancy-related hypertension, obstructed labour and complications of unsafe abortion; the vast majority are preventable. For every woman who dies, perhaps as many as 200 or 300 more survive to suffer from chronic illness or physical impairment; the number varies from country to country.

The major factor in preventing maternal morbidity and mortality is access to appropriate health services, including family planning. Pregnancy can be made much safer with technologies currently within reach of all countries. Emergency obstetric care, in particular, can save countless lives. Providing high-quality family planning and prenatal and delivery care for all women is among the goals of the Safe Motherhood Initiative, a global effort to improve women's health and to reduce maternal mortality by half by the year 2000.

El Salvador is working to make motherhood safer by training health promoters and traditional birth attendants, strengthening the nutritional component of its health care system and upgrading its maternal care referral system. In the Gambia, where maternal mortality rates are among the world's highest, the focus is on increasing the supervision and support of traditional birth attendants by health system personnel.

Worldwide, more than 40 million women are estimated to have abortions each year. Between 26 and 31 million are performed legally, and about 20 million are performed under unsafe conditions, accounting for an estimated 67,000 deaths. An even larger number of women suffer long-term complications such as infection, pain and infertility. In some countries, adolescents account for as much as 60 per cent of those hospitalized with abortion complications. The ICPD Programme of Action states that abortion must not be promoted as a method of family planning. It calls on Governments to deal with unsafe abortion as a major public health concern and to reduce recourse to abortion through expanded and improved family planning services.

Reproductive tract infections, sexually transmitted diseases and HIV/AIDS: Both women and men are vulnerable to a variety of reproductive tract infections; most are transmitted via sexual intercourse. Biologically, women are more vulnerable than men to sexual transmission of infections; their low status in many countries plays a major role in the prevalence of reproductive tract infections. If untreated, such infections can cause infertility or even death. This danger is greatest where services for diagnosis and treatment are limited, and where health workers and the public are not well-informed.

Early diagnosis and treatment of lower-reproductive-tract infections is the cheapest and most effective way to prevent more serious upper-tract infections. Some 250 million people contract a sexually transmitted disease each year, including 1 in 20 teenagers, and the number is increasing. Infected women are often left untreated, leading to ectopic pregnancy, chronic pain, genital tract cancer and complications during pregnancy and delivery.

By the end of 1994, more than 1 million cases of acquired immune deficiency syndrome (AIDS) had been officially recorded, and the actual total including undiagnosed cases was estimated at 4.5 million. A cumulative total of 19.5 million people had been infected with HIV, the virus that causes AIDS, since the late 1970s, including 1.5 million children. Between 13 and 15 million of those infected are believed to be still alive. The number of HIV-positive people is expected to reach 40 million by the year 2000. An estimated 1.5 million people became infected with HIV in the second half of 1994, the vast majority in less developed countries. About the same numbers of men and women were affected, but the number of infections among women is increasing faster than among men. The AIDS epidemic has placed a serious strain on the already overstretched health care systems in several developing countries. Male condoms are currently the most effective method for protection against many sexually transmitted diseases, including HIV/AIDS.

Family planning: In the past 20 years, many countries have dramatically expanded the availability of family planning services, accelerating a decline in fertility rates. An estimated 57 per cent of couples in developing countries now use contraceptives, compared to around 14 per cent in 1965-1970. The total fertility rate in developing countries has declined from 6.1 children per woman in the 1950s to 3.7 today. Female sterilization, oral contraceptives and IUDs account for most use of modern methods.

Practising family planning significantly reduces pregnancy-related mortality, primarily by reducing the overall number of pregnancies and related complications. Reducing the risk of unwanted pregnancies also reduces maternal deaths by reducing the recourse to abortion. Enabling women to control their fertility gives them greater control of their lives, allowing young women to continue their education without, for example, having it interrupted or terminated by a pregnancy.

Over 95 per cent of people in the developing world live in countries that directly support family planning programmes. The average distances that women must travel to the nearest clinic providing family planning services vary greatly, ranging from 1 kilometre in Egypt to 19 in Uganda. In general, women have much better access to family planning services in urban areas than in rural areas. Experience shows that family planning programmes work best when they are part of, or closely linked to, broader programmes addressing closely related health needs, and when women are fully involved in the design, delivery, management and evaluation of services.

While Governments have an interest in making family planning services available, use of the services must be completely voluntary; as the ICPD Programme of Action emphasizes, coercion has no part to play.

Written in association with UNFPA.

THE GIRL CHILD

Girls face inequality everywhere, but in many countries they do not even get a fighting chance to lead healthy, productive lives. Instead, they are devalued as human beings from the day they are born—and even before. In countries where a preference for sons is strong, girls are often aborted or killed as infants. Harvard economist Amartya Sen estimated that, in 1990, 100 million fewer women were alive than had been projected by demographic studies. Abortion, infanticide and other practices harmful to girls were clearly implicated in the numbers of "missing women".

Millions of girls are raised in an environment of neglect, overwork and often abuse, simply because they are female. In many countries girls are fed less than their brothers, forced to work harder, provided less schooling and denied equal access to medical care. They marry earlier and face greater risks of dying in adolescence and early adulthood because of early and too closely spaced pregnancies. Their impaired health and lost opportunities exact a terrible toll on society and on future generations.

Educating girls educates nations

"When I was little, I wasn't allowed to go to school", says Chichani, a Nepalese mother of four daughters. "I was married when I was 13." Like many girls in developing countries, Chichani, now 32, had to take on adult responsibilities and duties when she was just four or five years old. She took care of her younger siblings, cleaned the house, cooked the food, fetched water and wood and helped out in the fields, among other tasks. There wasn't much time left over for school or games in a childhood that ended definitively when Chichani entered into an early arranged marriage.

Discrimination and heavy workloads at home keep many more girls than boys out of school.

Statistics underscore their lost educational opportunities:

- *86 million girls—43 million more than boys—have no access to primary-school education.*

- *Approximately 500 million children start primary school, but more than 100 million children, two thirds of them girls, drop out before completing four years of primary school.*

- *Of the world's 1 billion illiterate adults, two thirds are women.*

Discrimination against girls in education prevails in many developing countries, but plagues industrialized countries as well. According to a 1992 report of the American Association of University Women, "School is still a place of unequal opportunity, where girls face discrimination from teachers, in textbooks, in tasks and from their male classmates." Girls receive less attention from teachers, read gender-biased textbooks and are excluded from many male-dominated fields of study.

Inferior education lowers a girl's self-esteem, her employment opportunities and her ability to take part in the world around her. Moreover, a girl's disadvantages are often passed on to her children later in life. Numerous studies have revealed that illiterate mothers whose lives are characterized by poverty and gender-based discrimination have daughters who are likely to share a similar destiny.

On the other hand, the advantages of educating mothers are indisputable. Women with schooling tend to delay marriage and childbirth and have fewer children. They also provide their children with better health and nutrition.

This cyclical effect points to a pressing need to improve the conditions of both girls and women. Just as elevating the status of women will ultimately help remove barriers that impede the growth and development of girls, investment in the welfare of girls will lead to improvement in the status of women.

Fortunately, a programme dedicated to improving the status of rural women in Nepal has helped Chichani improve her lot. Through a project called Production Credit for Rural Women, carried out by the Government of Nepal with support from UNICEF, she took out a loan to buy goats and vegetable seeds, and has installed a labour-saving stove in her house. The project has helped her learn to read and write and earn enough money to send her four daughters to school. "My daughters don't want to get married early", she explains. "They want to get an education."

Together, Governments, UN agencies and non-governmental organizations (NGOs) have taken concrete steps to make schools more welcoming to girls. These steps include bringing schools closer to communities, hiring more female teachers, devising meaningful and gender-sensitive curricula, lowering school costs and encouraging girls' participation.

Girls' health and nutrition: second-class fare

Education is not the only area in which girls are short-changed. In places where family resources are scarce and discrimination strong, girls get inferior food and health care. In many countries, girls are breast-fed for shorter periods than boys. A study in India, for instance, revealed that 51 per cent of boys were breast-fed, compared with 30 per cent of girls.

In addition, girls in many parts of the world are taken less often to health centres, have lower rates of immunization and receive less nurturing than their brothers. The inferior care they receive shows up in higher mortality statistics: in Colombia, for every 75 boys under the age of two who die, 100 girls die; in Bangladesh, India and Pakistan, every sixth death of a female infant is due to neglect and discrimination.

A girl's poor health and nutritional status may have consequences that last a lifetime. Iron-deficiency anaemia, for example, an affliction resulting from poor eating habits, affects beween 75 and 95 per cent of girls 15 or older in Africa. It is responsible for 20 per cent of all maternal deaths.

Moreover, a girl's poor health is likely to be passed on to the next generation when she becomes a mother, especially if she is uneducated. A United Nations study of 115 countries found that a mother's literacy was more closely correlated with life expectancy at birth than was any other factor. And a mother's education has a greater effect on lowering infant mortality and improving family health than does a father's education.

The adolescent girl: married with children

"It's very difficult and hard ... and painful to have a baby", says Joan, a 16-year-old Jamaican girl, who is pregnant. One of the most painful steps for Joan was dropping out of school and missing out on friends and social activities. Quitting school is a big problem for girls in Jamaica and the Caribbean in general, where 20 per cent of babies are born to teenagers.

In the Caribbean, poverty, peer pressure and poor sex counselling lead many girls to early marriage or pregnancy. In other regions of the world, including parts of Africa, the Middle East and South Asia, the devaluing of girls forces them to marry early and have many babies to increase their chance of having sons. In some African countries, for example, 50 per cent of women give birth before age 20.

No matter where they live, teenage girls who become pregnant and have babies increase their risk of developing infections and of dying during childbirth compared with women in their prime child-bearing years. Teenage mothers also expose their offspring to higher rates of disease and death than do older mothers. If they are illiterate, the risks are even higher.

Several statistics emphasize the hazards of early pregnancy and childbirth:

- *Pregnancy-related complications are the main cause of death for 15- to 19-year-old girls worldwide.*

- *Teenagers account for a quarter of the estimated 500,000 women who die each year from causes related to pregnancy and childbirth; 99 per cent of those deaths occur in the developing world.*

- *A baby born to a teenager 17 or younger has a 60 per cent greater chance of dying during the first year of life than a baby born to a mother 20 or older.*

- *Worldwide, one in every 20 teenagers acquires sexually transmitted diseases, including HIV/AIDS. For example, in Rwanda, a recent study revealed that 25 per cent of girls who became pregnant at 17 or younger were HIV-infected.*

13

Even if a teenager is not affected by disease, a young mother like Joan may lose out on education and employment opportunities that many of her friends take for granted.

But thanks to organizations like the Women's Centre Foundation of Jamaica, many teenagers are getting help. Founded in 1978, the Foundation, which receives support from the United Nations Population Fund and other local and international organizations, has provided counselling or vocational training to 11,000 young women whose average age is 14. With help from the Foundation, Joan hopes to enter sixth form at a local grammar school and later pursue an accounting career.

All work, no play

Nine-year-old Marceline is one of about a quarter-million "Cinderellas" who keep Haiti's homes running. These young servants, three quarters of whom are girls, are primarily the children of poor rural parents who can't afford to support them.

Marceline lives with her aunt and two cousins in Carrefour, a town on the outskirts of Port-au-Prince. She wakes at sunrise and fetches water. Then she buys food in the market and sweeps the house. Next she washes the dishes, while her cousins leave for school. In the evening, after her relatives eat dinner, she gets the leftovers. Finally she goes to sleep, on the floor under her aunt's bed.

Marceline is one of millions of children around the world who are victims of economic exploitation, working at jobs that threaten their health and well-being. Girls like Marceline are susceptible to economic exploitation, and there are millions of others who are even worse off. They face abuse, neglect and various forms of violence, sale, trafficking, abduction, torture and other deprivations of their basic rights and liberty.

While large numbers of girls work for long hours, both inside and outside the home, their labour is often unacknowledged and underrepresented in labour statistics. Several studies have shown substantial inequalities in gender distribution of household tasks and other chores among children:

- *Time allocation studies in Côte d'Ivoire indicate that, from age 10, women undertake 67 per cent of the work done by the combined male and female population.*

- *According to a government study in Nepal, the work burden of girls in both the 6-9 and 10-14 age groups is much heavier than that of boys in the same age groups in both rural and urban areas.*

- *Working girls face multiple job-related hazards. In match factories in India, girls often begin work at age 5 to 7 and labour 10 to 12 hours a day, seven days a week. Many are exposed to accidental fires and dangerous chemicals.*

- *Girls who work as domestic servants are extremely vulnerable to sexual abuse by their employers. A 1987 study of 100 families in Peru that employed house-girls found that 60 per cent of the adolescent males in the households had their first sexual encounter with the house-girls.*

14

Because financial difficulties often force both girls and boys to work, solutions to child labour must be linked to efforts aimed at eliminating poverty. Immediate steps to help child labourers should focus on making labour less exploitative of children's age and sex and more conducive to their overall development. Other initiatives might include government legislation and strict enforcement to protect the rights of girls in the home, workplace, school and playing-fields; greater recognition of the work of girls and women; non-formal training and education strategies to bring education to girls in the workplace; and provision of more creative and less exploitative environments for working girls.

In South Asia and other parts of the world, UNICEF is working with Governments, NGOs and the International Labour Organization, among other UN agencies, to protect children from exploitation and provide them with education in accordance with the Convention on the Rights of the Child.

On the streets

"After three months, I was completely demoralized", says Rosa, referring to her life as a 17-year-old Colombian prostitute. "I lost contact with my family and remained in that situation for many years."

Many girls like Rosa turn to the streets as a place to live to escape physical and sexual abuse or poverty. But the streets rarely offer a secure haven from their woes. Lacking permanent shelter and guardians, girls frequently become involved in prostitution, drug trafficking and petty crime. They also suffer several health-related problems, such as malnutrition and venereal disease.

At least 100 million children worldwide are believed to live at least part of the time on the streets.

Childhope USA, an international NGO trying to improve the lives of street children, estimates that girls constitute up to 30 per cent of street children in many developing countries. Helping some of Brazil's street children is SOS Crianca, an NGO that has emphasized peer counselling and training in personal health and safety.

When tradition is harmful

Over the past decade, female genital mutilation (FGM) has emerged as a primary focus of concern. This painful operation, carried out to preserve a girl's virginity and ensure her marriageability, endangers her physical and emotional health throughout her life.

According to the World Health Organization, about 2 million girls undergo FGM, or female circumcision, every year. The practice occurs in parts of Africa, the Middle East and Asia as well as in immigrant communities in Europe, North America and Australia.

The 1993 UN Declaration on the Elimination of Violence against Women identified FGM as an act of violence against girls. Its eradication will require long-term commitment

15

Time use of children in rural areas
Number of hours spent per day in different activities

	India, 1990				Nepal, 1990			
	Ages 6-9		Ages 10-14		Ages 6-9		Ages 10-14	
	Girls	Boys	Girls	Boys	Girls	Boys	Girls	Boys
Work	3.0	1.9	5.4	4.0	3.2	1.7	7.7	4.4
Non-subsistence	0.7	0.6	2.3	2.9	0.3	0.3	1.8	1.3
Subsistence	0.9	0.7	0.8	0.5	0.7	0.4	2.0	1.2
Household	1.4	0.7	2.3	0.6	2.2	1.0	4.0	2.0
Reading/studying	0.4	2.5	0.2	1.1	2.1	4.8	3.8	0.3
Leisure	1.3	1.5	0.8	1.2	—	—	—	—

Source: Compiled by the Statistical Division of the United Nations Secretariat from national studies.

and collaboration among Governments, development agencies, NGOs and, most importantly, the communities in the countries where it is practised. The Inter-African Committee (IAC) on Traditional Practices, headquartered in Geneva, and the Commission for the Abolition of Sexual Mutilation, headquartered in Paris and founded by a Senegalese woman, are two agencies leading the fight against FGM. IAC has more than 30 National Committees in Africa actively working against this practice.

A global agenda for girls

Several international treaties have drawn global support for the needs and rights of girls and women. The Convention on the Rights of the Child, the Declaration of the World Summit for Children in 1990 and the Convention on the Elimination of All Forms of Discrimination against Women in 1981 endorsed the right of girls and women to equal opportunities in health, education and employment. In addition, these treaties specifically protect children and women against all forms of exploitation and abuse.

Issues of equality and opportunity for girls and women were given high priority at the 1995 World Social Summit in Copenhagen and featured prominently at the Fourth World Conference on Women. These global commitments have been reaffirmed and strengthened by several regional declarations, including the seven-nation South Asian Association for Regional Cooperation (SAARC), which declared 1991-2000 "The Decade of the Girl Child".

It is up to Governments, individuals and communities to ensure that these declarations and promises translate into enforceable laws and policies that promote a better future for girls everywhere. An investment in girls is an investment in the future.

Written in association with UNICEF.

VIOLENCE AGAINST WOMEN

"Imagine a world in which three to four million people are suddenly struck by a serious, recurring illness. There is chronic pain, trauma and injury. Authorities fail to draw any connection between individual bouts with the disease and the greater public threat. Many suffer in silence."

The world that Joseph R. Biden, former chairman of the U.S. Senate Judiciary Committee, describes here is his own country, the United States of America, and the "disease" is domestic violence. The vast majority of victims are women. In the U.S., one woman is physically abused every eight seconds and one is raped every six minutes. Spouse abuse is more common in the U.S. than automobile accidents, mugging and cancer deaths combined, notes a 1992 U.S. Senate Judiciary Committee report.

Yet the seriousness or scope of the problem is often ignored. "If the leading newspapers were to announce tomorrow a new disease that, over the past year, had afflicted from 3 to 4 million citizens, few would fail to appreciate the seriousness of the illness. Yet, when it comes to the 3 to 4 million women who are victimized by violence each year, the alarms ring softly", said Senator Biden.

Violence against women, selected countries, around 1990

Source: Lori Heise, Pacific Institute for Women's Health, 1992

NORWAY	USA	THAILAND	PERU
25% of female gynaecological patients have been sexually abused by their partners	1 in 5 adult women has been raped	In the biggest slum in Bangkok, 50% of married women are beaten regularly	70% of all crimes reported to police are of women beaten by their husbands

A global phenomenon

Everywhere and in all ages, women have been victims of violence. They are and often have been raped, mutilated, battered and murdered.

In most societies, gender-based violence has long been tolerated, letting the perpetrators go unpunished, their crime tacitly condoned. Based on the popular view that a wife is the property of her husband and that therefore he may do with her whatever he thinks fit, legal systems in some countries have recognized a husband's right to chastise or even kill his wife if she is considered disobedient or is thought to have committed adultery. A parliamentarian in Papua New Guinea, taking part in a debate on wife battering, went as far as to say, "Wife beating is an accepted custom. We are wasting our time debating this issue."

Such violence is often covered by a veil of secrecy and denial. Rarely are gender-based abuses reported or recorded. In the U.S., according to a study published in *American Psychologist*, only 2 per cent of intrafamilial child sexual abuse, 6 per cent of extrafamilial sexual abuse and 5 to 8 per cent of adult sexual assault cases are reported to the police. However, with increased awareness it is now possible to see how widespread and multifaceted the situation is. This is evident from various recent studies, including a 1994 World Bank discussion paper on violence against women.

- Studies from a variety of countries show that one quarter to more than half of women report having been physically abused by a present or former partner. Far more are subjected to ongoing emotional and psychological abuse.

- Sexual abuse is not only common but widespread in most countries. In Canada, a 1993 study based on 420 randomly selected women found that more than 54 per cent of them had experienced some form of unwanted or intrusive sexual experience before reaching the age of 16; 51 per cent reported being victims of rape or attempted rape. In 25 per cent of the cases, women who were physically assaulted reported that their partners explicitly threatened to kill them.

- Rape during war is still common. According to a European Union fact-finding team, 20,000 women were raped in Bosnia in the first months of the war. Similarly, women have been raped in recent years in civil strifes in Cambodia, Liberia, Peru, Somalia and Uganda.

- Girl-children and adolescents continue to be abused in many countries. In Barbados, one woman in three and one to two men in 100 report being sexually abused during childhood or adolescence. In Peru, a study found 90 per cent of the young mothers aged 12 to 16 in a hospital to be rape victims, often as a result of assault by a father, stepfather or other close relative. In Costa Rica, 95 per cent of pregnant clients under 15 at a hospital were found to be incest victims.

18

- Dowry-related abuse is common in some countries. In India, where "bride burning" is a known practice, official police records show that 4,835 women were killed in 1990 due to the failure of their families to meet demands for money and goods. In greater Bombay, one of every five deaths among women aged 15 to 44 was reported to be a case of "accidental burns".

- Female infanticide and selective abortion of female foetuses has increased in several Asian countries. Female infants are often killed within a few days of birth. In a South Asian country, one study over a two-and-a-half-year period found that 58 per cent of known female infanticide was committed by feeding babies the poisonous sap of a plant or by choking them by lodging rice hulls soaked in milk in their throats.

- Genital mutilation, a traditional practice affecting women's health, is practised in parts of Africa and Asia, and among immigrants in the U.S. and Europe. Globally, at least 2 million girls a year experience genital mutilation, approximately 6,000 new cases every day—five girls every minute.

- Women are at greater risk of violence and resulting injury in their homes and from men they know. At a police station in São Paulo, Brazil, 70 per cent of all reported cases of violence against women had taken place in the home. In Santiago, Chile, almost three quarters of all assault-related injuries to women were found to be caused by family members. In Canada, 62 per cent of women murdered in 1987 died at the hands of their spouses.

- Violence during pregnancy is identified as a major reason for miscarriage and low-birth-weight children. In Mexico City, a survey of 342 randomly sampled women found that 20 per cent of those battered reported blows to the stomach. In Costa Rica, 49 per cent of a group of 80 battered women reported having been beaten during pregnancy; 7.5 per cent of them reported miscarriages.

Why women are at risk

"A wife married is like a pony bought. I will ride her and whip her as I like."

This proverb, no matter how old, is still relevant. Whether it is beating a wife at the end of a bad day or preying on an unsuspecting evening jogger at a city park, most gender-based violence against women is inextricably linked to male power, privilege and control. Culture and tradition, often reflected in national laws, only help to perpetuate the idea of male dominance.

Excessive use of alcohol and drugs has been identified as a factor behind gender abuse. Economic and social factors, such as unemployment, economic stress, overcrowding and unfavourable and frustrating work conditions, also lead to gender-based violence. Some researchers have also argued that violence is actually a learned behaviour. Today's violent husbands are yesterday's children of violent parents, they say. In fact, as one study in the U.S. found, men who saw their parents attack each other,

19

compared with those from non-violent families of origin, were three times more likely to hit their wives and ten times more likely to attack them with a weapon.

Men accused of violence against their wives sometimes try to shift the blame, claiming their actions were provoked by the behaviour of their partners. Upon close examination, researchers discovered that such behaviour was often linked to some form of failure or refusal on the part of the women to comply with or support their husbands' wishes and authority. As a study in the *British Journal of Crime* noted, to a violent husband/partner, almost anything seemed to be provocative: "being too talkative or too quiet, too sexual or not sexual enough, too frugal or too extravagant, too often pregnant or not frequently enough".

In some countries, drunkenness is accepted by the judiciary as a defence in assaults against women. In September 1994, the Supreme Court in Canada overturned the conviction of a man who, having consumed a large amount of alcohol, pulled a 65-year-old woman out of a wheelchair and sexually assaulted her.

A more universal reason behind gender-based violence, many people think, is the structural inequality between men and women in the family as well as in society. Studies from both developed and developing countries show violence against women to be a by-product of the societal structure in which men make all decisions and women are expected to obey.

Whether within the family or outside it, women's lower status manifests itself in an overall acceptance of abusive or violent conduct towards women as "normal". As a United Nations study on domestic violence concludes, violence against women is a function of the belief, fostered in all cultures, that men are superior and that the women they live with are their possessions or chattels, which they may treat as they wish and as they consider appropriate.

- Commenting on her husband, the wife of a Nobel Peace Prize winner once said, "He is a good husband; he only hits me once a week."

The health consequences

"My ex-husband shot me through the head as I slept and left me for dead. I managed to walk downstairs, where my daughter was calling for help. My husband proceeded to stab me with such force that the knife-tip broke off in my intestines. He robbed me of my eyesight, my sense of taste and smell. He robbed me of my family and my stepchildren."

This unidentified woman, who gave testimony to a Canadian panel on violence against women, is just one of the numerous victims of gender-based violence who have to live with scars on their bodies and fear in their minds. According to a report of the Global Commission on Women's Health, in addition to morbidity and mortality, violence against women leads to psychological trauma, depression, substance abuse, injuries, sexually transmitted diseases and HIV infection, suicide and murder. This places an enormous financial burden on the national health-care system.

The World Bank, in its 1993 *World Development Report*, for the first time assessed the health consequences of gender-based violence. Based on the limited data available, it estimated that in industrialized countries rape and domestic violence take away almost one in every five healthy years of life of women aged 15 to 44. On a per capita basis, the health burden of domestic violence is about the same for reproductive-age women in both developed and developing countries.

However, since malnutrition and poverty-related diseases are widespread in developing countries, the overall health burden there is greater. As a result, the percentage of health burden attributable to gender-based violence victimization is smaller, about 5 per cent. But in some developing countries where maternal mortality and poverty-related diseases have been brought under relative control, the healthy years of life lost to rape and domestic violence appear as a larger percentage—16 per cent of the total burden.

An obstacle to development

Women's participation in the development process—especially in areas such as family planning, environmental protection and education—is crucial. Yet when women are faced with violence, their ability to participate fully in these and other aspects of development is hampered. In many countries, husbands resist women's work outside the home, since they fear this may lead to women's empowerment. Men often use force or threats in order to divert or extort women's income.

- The Women's Development Programme in Rajasthan, India, was sponsored by the Government, but its success was due largely to the energy and drive of its leader, a young woman. One of the goals of the Programme was to reduce child marriage. The campaign, though popular among women and certain segments of society, angered many people, including some village elders. One day the programme leader's home was raided by a group of men. She was gang-raped by them in front of her husband. As she lay unconscious, the leader of the gang told her horror-stricken husband, "Keep your wife in line or we will rape her again." This virtually ended a successful programme aimed at improving the lives of girls and women.

A society may eventually quantify its economic loss due to gender-based violence, but how can it ever calculate the loss it suffers due to the fact that women are not safe and their freedom is restricted?

Combating violence: move for a global agenda

Though violence against women is as old as human civilization, it became a matter of international concern only after the 1985 third world conference on women, in Nairobi. The UN-sponsored Conference was notable for the adoption of the Strategies for the Advancement of Women to the Year 2000. This document, which provided a

21

framework for action at the national, regional and international levels, identified violence against women as a major obstacle to the achievement of the three objectives of the UN Women's Decade 1976-1985: equality, development and peace. It called for legal measures to prevent gender-based violence and to set up national machineries to deal with the question.

In June 1993, the World Conference on Human Rights, in Vienna, Austria, stressed the importance of working towards the elimination of violence against women in public and private life. One outcome of the Conference was the appointment of a Special UN Rapporteur on violence against women. The Rapporteur, who looks into causes and consequences of violence against women and recommends ways and means to eliminate them, reports to the UN Commission on Human Rights on an annual basis.

In December 1993, the General Assembly adopted the Declaration on the Elimination of Violence against Women. This Declaration defines for the first time what constitutes an act of violence against women and calls on Governments and the international community to take specific measures to prevent such acts.

In September 1995, at the Fourth World Conference on Women, the world will have an opportunity to review and appraise the advancement of women since the UN held its first conference on women two decades ago. The Conference is expected to adopt a Platform for Action that will spell out actions Governments and communities can take to make the Nairobi Forward-looking Strategies a reality. Violence against Women is one of the 12 critical areas of concern identified in the Draft Platform.

A Platform for Action

"Violence against women derives essentially from the lower status accorded to women in the family and in society. It is abetted by ignorance, lack of laws to prohibit violence, inadequate efforts by public authorities to enforce existing laws, and absence of educational and other means to address its causes", says an initial version of the Draft

Platform for Action. Experience in a number of countries shows that women and men can be mobilized to fight against violence in all its forms and that effective public measures can be taken to address both the consequences and the causes of violence.

The Draft Platform proposes specific measures Governments and communities can take to eliminate violence against women.

These include:

1. *Recognize violence against women as a violation of women's human rights;*
2. *Cooperate with the Special UN Rapporteur on Violence against Women;*
3. *Study and widely publicize root causes and mechanisms of different forms of violence against women;*
4. *Analyze and review existing laws relevant to violence against women and develop new legislative efforts, in accordance with the Declaration on Violence against Women;*
5. *Address both the causes and the consequences of violence against women, using both legal and social measures. Emphasize preventing violence as well as protecting women subject to violence;*
6. *Launch legal literacy programmes and information campaigns on existing laws and women's human rights;*
7. *Include in the curricula material on gender inequality and violence;*
8. *Train the judiciary and the police to ensure fair treatment of women targets of violence, increase recruitment of women into the police forces and ensure higher representation of women in the judiciary;*
9. *Set up high-level national bodies to oversee the working of safeguards for women;*
10. *Take specific action to protect women and girls who are subjects of sex trafficking and forced prostitution;*
11. *Take special measures to protect women with disabilities and female migrant workers.*

Taking away the excuse

Any act of violence is actually the use of coercive forms of power. It is used to compel someone to do something he or she is unwilling to do. Violence against women is clearly a way to ensure their subordination to men. An essential step in combating violence against women is to take away any excuse. No coercive use of power can be considered legitimate under any circumstances.

To stop violence against women, each society needs to look at itself and to challenge those values and beliefs that reinforce male violence. Experts taking part in an October 1993 meeting on violence against women organized by the UN's Division for the Advancement of Women felt that each type of violence required its own remedy. Some solutions might come through the legal system and the police function of the State. Others might require the use of public institutions, like the educational system, to influence values and attitudes. Still others might require opinion leadership by community leaders and the mass media. Acceptance of responsibility publicly to shame persons who violate the norm of no violence can also be an effective measure.

As the experts concluded, "rather than the punishment fitting the crime, it is more a matter of the prevention fitting the cause".

Defining violence against women

In December 1993, the United Nations General Assembly adopted a landmark resolution on gender violence called the Declaration on the Elimination of Violence against Women. It defined violence as "any act of gender-based violence that results in, or is likely to result in, physical, sexual or psychological harm or suffering to women, including threat of such acts, coercion or arbitrary deprivations of liberty, whether occuring in public or private life".

The Declaration also lists abuses that fall into the category of violence against women:

1. Physical, sexual, and psychological violence occuring in the family and in the community, including battering, sexual abuse of female children, dowry-related violence, marital rape, female genital mutilation and other traditional practices harmful to women;
2. Non-spousal violence;
3. Violence related to exploitation;
4. Sexual harassment and intimidation at work, in educational institutions and elsewhere;
5. Trafficking in women;
6. Forced prostitution; and
7. Violence perpetrated or condoned by the State.

Though very broad-based and comprehensive, this definition, according to some women's rights advocates and analysts, includes only acts perpetrated by an individual or the State and excludes laws, policies or structural inequalities that could be considered as violent. Lori Heise, a Director at the Pacific Insitute for Women's Health, in Washington D.C., writing in association with Jacqueline Pitanguy and Adrienne Germain, said in a World Bank study that the UN definition provides insufficient guidance to determine whether items that are not listed, such as female foeticide or restrictive abortion policies, would constitute gender violence. Any definition of violence, said Ms.Heise, must have at its centre the core concepts of force and coercion, which distinguish between violent and merely oppressive behaviour.

Ms. Heise and her associates have come up with their own definition of violence against women: any act of verbal or physical force, coercion, or life-threatening deprivation, directed at an individual woman or girl, that causes physical or psychological harm, humiliation or arbitrary deprivation of liberty and that perpetuates female subordination.

"That was a way of life, and it was not right"

American football is different from soccer, which is better known as football in most part of the world. But when it comes to the emotions that they evoke, there is no difference between the two.

Troy Vincent is a cornerback for the Miami Dolphins football team. He is rich and famous now, but as a child he had to watch helplessly as his mother was abused. "To see my mother get beat was the way of life in my home. It was part of the community to beat your wife. When you would leave home and go to school, you would hear some of the guys say, 'Man, I smacked my girlfriend three times last night.' Then one of his friends gave him a high five. That was a way of life, and it was not right."

Mr. Vincent admitted seeing his mother in the morning with a cast on her arm, but did not know how he could help her. "It is very disturbing to see a woman be a prisoner in her own home", he said. Mr. Vincent was joined by several other famous athletes who took part in a panel discussion on domestic violence in Florida in October 1994. All of them had similar stories to tell.

Stephen Braggs, also a star player for the Dolphins, admitted that he often mentally abused his wife because he was a perfectionist. "I would practice mental abuse, like, 'Why are you always fat? You have never been anything. Why are you always doing this wrong?'"

Irving Fryer, another football star, admitted that he had abused his wife. It was now a matter of the past, he said, but this was something he continued to deal with emotionally. "We are all products of our environment. Some of the things that happened in my home, I had to practice to get away from. And it just didn't happen overnight", he said.

There is a simple conclusion to be drawn from all this: no one is born violent, but if children grow up amidst violence, they may end up being violent themselves. If violence against women is to be stopped, it must end where it begins, in the family.

Based on a report published in The New York Times.

WOMEN AND AIDS

Eight years ago, when Chris Kaleeba lay dying of AIDS in a hospital outside London, his wife Noerine kept vigil by his bedside. He had contracted the disease through a blood transfusion. For four months their only source of comfort was the staff of Castle Hill Hospital.

As Chris's condition worsened, they returned to Uganda because he wanted to die in his homeland. They were not prepared for what was in store. "There really wasn't much support in Uganda except from both sides of the family", says Mrs. Kaleeba. "We had emotional support but we lacked medicine and material goods. We were also stigmatized by friends and neighbours."

Mrs. Kaleeba was devastated when Chris died. But she was even more determined to do something to help people with HIV/AIDS and their families. In November 1987 she founded The AIDS Support Organization (TASO), a non-governmental organization, to help Ugandans "live positively with AIDS".

TASO provides AIDS education, counselling and medicine to over 5,000 people with HIV infection or AIDS and to their families. It also provides food, clothing and other material support and free HIV testing. In addition, TASO helps people with HIV/AIDS and their relatives initiate income-generating activities. It trains counsellors and health educators and mobilizes communities to care for their sick. Many TASO staff and volunteers are themselves people with HIV or AIDS.

Mrs Kaleeba is just one example of women coming forward to help combat the consequences of this killer disease. Wives, grandmothers, mothers, sisters and daughters the world over are caring for people with AIDS and for their survivors, even when they themselves have been diagnosed HIV-positive. Women are running orphanages, hospices and soup kitchens for AIDS patients and their families.

No longer a "man's disease"

While women are now at the centre of helping to offset the impact of HIV/AIDS, they are also particularly susceptible to HIV infection. As more women become infected, so too do more infants through perinatal transmission. The majority of infected women are not aware of their condition. They are often diagnosed after becoming pregnant or giving birth.

In some countries, AIDS was long considered to be a "homosexual man's disease". Only a decade or so ago, women were thought to be on the periphery of the crisis. Today, they are at the centre of a growing epidemic.

According to the World Health Organization (WHO), more than 5 million women have been infected with HIV worldwide. Almost half of all newly infected adults are women. In 1993 alone, more than one million women were newly infected. WHO estimates that by the year 2000, nearly 15 million women will have become infected with HIV, and about 4 million of them will have died.

Of the over 18 million adults and adolescents worldwide now believed to be HIV-positive, one third are women of child-bearing age. "Women are twice as likely to contract the disease through a single exposure as men are", says Dr. Fathia Mahmoud, of the Africa-based Society for Women and AIDS.

AIDS among women in the developed countries is also on the rise. In 1983, 7 per cent of the AIDS cases reported by the US Centers for Disease Control were women. That figure increased to 13 per cent in 1994.

Though transmission of the AIDS virus through heterosexual contact has been predominant in many developing countries, transmission in industrialized countries is still often through homosexual contact or drug use. However, according to WHO, the rise in heterosexual transmission is ominous. In 1992, sex became the leading cause of AIDS in American women. In Scotland, a significant proportion of new HIV infections in some cities are acquired through sex between men and women. Drug injecting is the background to many of these infections, with women contracting the disease through sex with a male drug user.

Young and vulnerable

Young women are the group most susceptible to HIV infection. According to a United Nations Development Programme (UNDP) study on AIDS, seventy per cent of the 3,000 women a day who contract HIV and the 500 women who die daily from AIDS worldwide are between the ages of 15 and 25. The study, conducted in three African and two Asian countries, found:

In Thailand, the HIV infection rate is greater among women between the ages of 15 and 25 than among all other women combined.

In Uganda, more than twice as many reported AIDS cases are among 15- to 25-year-old women than among men of the same age.

In Rwanda, more than 25 per cent of women who become pregnant and about 17 per cent of those who engage in intercourse before they are 17 years old will become HIV-positive.

Dr. Michael Merson, Executive Director of the WHO Global Programme on AIDS, has listed three causes for high infection rates in young women:

26

- *Women are biologically more vulnerable. As the receptive partner, women have a larger mucosal surface exposed during sexual intercourse; moreover, semen contains a far higher concentration of HIV than vaginal fluid. Women thus run a bigger risk of acquiring HIV infection—and other sexually transmitted diseases.*

- *Women are epidemiologically vulnerable. Women tend to marry or have sex with older men, who may have more sexual partners and hence be more likely to have become infected. Women are also epidemiologically vulnerable to HIV transmission through blood. In the developing world, women frequently require a blood transfusion during pregnancy or childbirth—for example, because of anaemia or haemorrhage.*

- *Women are socially vulnerable to HIV. Men are expected to be assertive and women passive in their sexual relationships. In some cultures, men expect sex with any woman receiving their economic support. Whenever these traditional norms predominate, the result is sexual subordination, and this creates a highly unfavourable atmosphere for AIDS prevention.*

When subordination leads to disaster

Women's sexual subordination is a direct result of their lower status in society, lack of independent income and lack of control over their sexual and economic lives. This dependency only heightens women's vulnerability to HIV infection.

In many societies, girls are married at an early age. They are also the most frequent victims of incest and rape. Non-consensual, hurried or frequent intercourse can inhibit mucus production and cause genital trauma, increasing the likelihood of

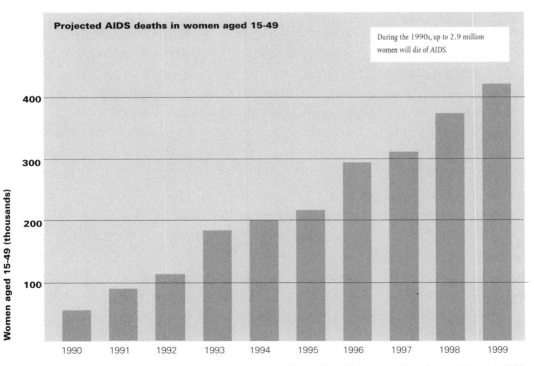

Projected AIDS deaths in women aged 15-49

During the 1990s, up to 2.9 million women will die of AIDS.

Source: *Social Science and Medicine*, vol. 31, No. 6, 1990

infection. Young women's lack of control over the circumstances under which intercourse occurs thus puts them at greater risk of HIV infection. Men often prefer to have sexual relations with younger women, who are assumed to be sexually inactive and thereby "safe" from HIV. This also places these girls at high risk of infection.

In the UNDP study on AIDS, several women said that they dared not deny a husband his "conjugal rights" even when they knew that he was engaging in risky sexual behaviour. To do so might result in divorce or abandonment. The same African women and their Asian sisters confessed an unwillingness to broach the subject of condom use with their husbands for fear of similar repercussions.

The chance of infection is also higher for women with genital lesions, inflammation or secretions. These may be caused by infections, sexual activity or such traditional practices as infibulation, the most extreme form of female circumcision. Women have limited or no access to information, diagnostic facilities and treatment for these conditions, including sexually transmitted diseases. Women's lower literacy rates and restricted mobility only make them more vulnerable.

From mother to child: the cord that binds

Women often face the agony of transmitting the virus to their babies in the womb, during birth or while breast-feeding. Up to one third of infants born to infected mothers may be HIV-positive. By the end of 1993, close to 1 million HIV-infected babies had been born in Africa. By the year 2000, an additional 2 to 3 million are expected to be infected.

High levels of infection are found in pregnant women in developed countries in certain settings. According to the Centers for Disease Control and Prevention, surveys of women attending reproductive health and other clinics in 1991-1992 in certain parts of the United States have found high rates of HIV infection, including up to 1.4 per cent in Newark (New Jersey), 1.7 per cent in Miami (Florida), 2.3 per cent in New York and 3.3 per cent in Boston (Massachusetts). In some maternity hospitals in Paris, seroprevalence rates approach 1 per cent.

Too poor to fight

Poverty and other factors often force women into commercial sex, significantly increasing their risk of infection. In some Asian countries, levels of HIV infection among prostitutes are increasing rapidly, with a rate of 70 per cent in some areas.

Prostitution is an illegal but powerful sex-service industry in these countries, catering to millions of Asian men and foreign tourists. Because a prostitute has an average of five clients a day, the rate of HIV transmission from clients to sex workers and from sex workers to clients and, in turn, to their wives or partners is high.

The epidemic has caused extreme hardships for prostitutes. They are afraid of risking death from the virus, but have no comparable means of earning income to support themselves, their children, elderly parents and other relatives. Many would like to protect themselves through condom use but cannot enforce this if a client refuses. Moreover, clients have been known to pay more for sex without a condom, which they claim is more pleasurable.

The situation was best explained by an Asian woman: "AIDS might make me sick one day, but if I don't work, my family would not eat and we would all be sick anyway."

In developed countries, too, poorer women are among those most affected. According to a recent study, U.S. women with AIDS are poorer than the general population, and 73 per cent of them are African-American or Hispanic—compared with 40 per cent of men with AIDS.

Projected distribution of HIV-infected women (excluding AIDS cases) in 1995

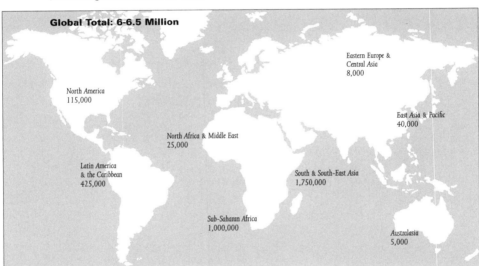

Source: WHO Global Programme on AIDS, April 1994

Setting priorities

Though women are at the centre of a growing HIV epidemic, the national and international response to this major health issue is weak and inadequate. For women, mothers and children, large gaps exist between needs—medical, psychological and welfare—and services or support to meet those needs. Nor is sufficient effort directed towards policy development. Policies on HIV-infected pregnant women, for example, do not generally take into account reproductive rights. Screening policies are discussed without considering the capacity of the prenatal-care system. Economic factors are not often considered while discussing prostitution. Most importantly, women are rarely involved in the formulation of AIDS policies. As in most other health and social issues, policies on AIDS are "made by men—for men".

29

According to the UNDP study, in developing a global strategy to respond to the special needs of women, two essential elements need to be addressed. First, the silence around the infection of young women must be challenged at every level: individual, family, community and organization, national and international. Girls and young women must be able to speak out, to cease feeling silenced or powerless to change what happens to them. When women affected by the HIV virus are able to break the wall of silence surrounding them, society will be under pressure to confront the existing reality and adopt policies to respond.

Secondly, a new research agenda must be established. Not enough is known about AIDS. Nor is what is already known widely disseminated. A focused effort must be made to support continued bioscientific research. In addition to scientists and doctors, nurses and social workers should be made partners in the process of determining the research agenda.

An agenda for action

WHO and UNDP in a joint study have suggested specific measures that Governments, communities and individuals can take to reduce the vulnerability of women to HIV/AIDS, including:

Preventing HIV infection among girls and women: Increase girls' access to education, support HIV/AIDS education for young people in and out of school, encourage safer sex with the use of condoms, and increase women's access to economic activities. To reduce the incidence and prevalence of sexually transmitted diseases (STD), increase women's access to and utilization of appropriate STD services.

Reducing the impact of HIV/AIDS on women: Encourage countries to replace routine HIV screening with voluntary/confidential testing, support family and community-based work with HIV/AIDS infected women, review laws and regulations on prostitution and work conditions of prostitutes.

Caring for women with HIV/AIDS: Ensure access to voluntary, safe and affordable contraceptive measures, support women with HIV/AIDS in family-planning decisions, ensure that women with HIV/AIDS infection are not pressured into terminating pregnancies. To ensure that women do not carry the entire burden of care for people with HIV/AIDS, encourage men and women to share in care-giving roles.

Women with AIDS: Putting them on the global agenda since the first world conference on women, held in Mexico City in 1975, women's health issues have started receiving global attention. In Copenhagen, at the second women's conference, in 1980, and in Nairobi, at the third conference, in 1985, the vital role women play as health-care providers was fully recognized. The Forward-looking Strategies for the Advancement of Women to the Year 2000, adopted at the Nairobi Conference as a framework for action for improving women's status, urged actions to identify and reduce risks to women's health and called for promoting "the positive health of women at all stages of life".

30

A common agenda and a common goal

The world is yet to realize fully the special threat that AIDS poses to women. Combating this threat involves much more than improving women's health conditions. As long as women are discriminated against and cultural and legal barriers obstruct their decision-making and choices, women will remain vulnerable to HIV infection. The linkages between women's status in society and the danger they face from HIV infection have to be recognized and fought against.

"Can we meet the intricate challenges presented to our era by this painful new disease?" asked James Grant, former Executive Director of the United Nations Children's Fund (UNICEF). His answer: "Working together, I think we can."

Dying young

"My name is Ali Gertz, I am 23 years old and I have AIDS. A while back I slept with a man, I slept with him one night. That was all and I got ill."

This is from the public service announcement Alison Gertz made in 1990 for radio before she died of AIDS. An only child of affluent New Yorkers, she was a rather unlikely candidate for this deadly disease. She had never used drugs intravenously. She was not promiscuous and had never had a blood transfusion. Her illness was traced back to one sexual encounter she had had seven years earlier. She was then 16 years old and involved with an older man. This man had since died of AIDS, something Alison had known nothing about.

"After the initial shock, the first thought that came to my mind was that I was going to die. But at the same time I didn't feel that this was true. I felt like two different people, one whose life was over, and the other, the positive, optimistic person that I am. I said I am going to fight back", Alison recalled.

A few months after learning that she had AIDS, and after discussing it with her parents, Alison decided to go public. She thought this way she could help other people to avoid the disease. Alison appeared on TV and radio programmes. She received hundreds of letters from people, some of them in the same situation as herself.

Alison set up an organization called "Love Heals". "I decided that this was to be my vocation in life, to help people who are sick and don't have as much support as I do. Another reason for setting it up was public awareness."

In her speeches and press interviews, in meetings with students and young women, Alison tried to clear up the many misconceptions people have about AIDS. One cannot become infected with AIDS by sharing knives and forks or by casual kissing, nor from toilet seats, public transport, sneezing or shaking hands, or any casual contact. The disease is spread through sexual intercourse, exposure to contaminated blood or from an infected mother to a child. She also urged young people to be more responsible. "You should be more careful about what you are doing and when you are doing it", she said.

One year later, Alison died. She died so young because she did not know about AIDS when she contracted the deadly virus. Others don't have to suffer a similar fate because they can learn how to prevent it.

(Based on "Alison", a video produced by WHO. For copies, please contact: World Health Organization, Distribution and Sales, 1211 Geneva 27, Switzerland)

Written in association with UNDP.

WOMEN AND THE ENVIRONMENT

by Bella Abzug

Clean air and water. Fertile soil. Easy access to replenishable sources of non-toxic food, fuel and energy. Preservation of biodiversity in natural resources, lakes, rivers, oceans, forests, plant and animal species. Sustainable development. Protection of our ancient, beautiful, increasingly vulnerable planet from a plague of man-made pollutants, new technologies and economic practices that adversely affect the rights, health and lives of Earth's inhabitants.

Add to their belief in these elemental life-preserving principles the belief that women can make a difference, and we have the remarkable story of how in the closing years of the 20th century women of every class, colour and culture have emerged as a powerful organized force for positive change around the world. Everywhere, women are catalysts and initiators of environmental and democratic activism, demanding an equal voice in "fate of the Earth" decisions and an end to the poverty and exploitative development patterns that often primarily victimize women and children.

As individuals and in thousands of new as well as long-established women's organizations, ranging from community groups to international networks, women are bringing their unique life experiences, concerns, perspectives and holistic analyses into the processes through which the United Nations, Governments, international finance, transnational corporations, public and private institutions shape policies that affect their lives.

Women as natural resource managers

Women have joined the global debate on environment from a broad range of entry points. Their involvement may take the form of transforming simple household chores, such as women in Yemen do by re-using scarce water ... or planting 10 million trees in Africa's innovative Green Belt Movement, initiated by Wangari Maathai of Kenya, to combat desertification and provide income for poor women ... recycling garbage and cleaning up polluted lakes and rivers, as women in the United States, Canada and Europe do ... risking their lives in civil disobedience as the Chipko women tree-huggers in India did to save the local forest on which their livelihoods depend ...

Division of labour

■ Men	Ploughing 30%	Harvesting 60%	
	Planting 50%	Weeding 70%	
▨ Women	Livestock 50%	Processing & storing crops 85%	
		Domestic work 95%	

Women in Africa do up to three quarters of all agricultural work in addition to their domestic responsibilities.

Source: UN Economic Commission for Africa

organizing demonstrations against toxic dumps and nuclear tests ... opposing expulsion of indigenous people from their traditional lands ... or using their expertise as scientists, technologists, economists and educators have done to devise alternative environment- and people-friendly models of development ... and, as physicist Vandana Shiva of India has done, to launch an international campaign against genetic engineering of seeds and food by transnational corporations, a practice that she charges deprives local food growers of their property rights and sustainable approach to agriculture and exposes consumers to health risks. Women have moved into the forefront of environmental initiatives because they are typically the first to recognize environmental problems and are most directly affected by them. In Africa, Asia, Latin America and other developing regions, women are often the primary users and managers of land, forests, water and other natural resources.

About half the world's food is grown by women. In Africa they produce nearly all the food their families consume, while Asian and Latin American women typically carry out key stages of production and processing for staple crops and are the main producers of vegetables and livestock for the household. Thus they acquire important knowledge of local soil conditions, growing cycles and other environmental features and are able to use this knowledge for conservation. Women in the Andean regions of South America, for instance, maintain the seed banks on which the local crops depend. Gambian women grow most of the rice in their country and have initiated dike-building schemes and created vegetable plots to protect and enrich the local soil.

Throughout much of the developing world, women also have primary responsibility for gathering fuel, food and fodder from forest areas and for collecting and managing water. Women's traditional use of these natural resources has generally ensured their availability for future use. For example, rural women throughout India prefer to collect dead branches for fuelwood rather than cut down live trees.

But women often bear the worst consequences of industrial logging, commercial fishing and other activities that ignore the principle of sustainability. If large tracts of forests are destroyed, if fishing supplies dwindle, if water supplies dry up or are contaminated by pesticides, if huge dams are built, displacing thousands of families from their traditional homes, it is women who have to cope with the increased difficulties of day-to-day survival for their families. In Nepal, for example, women whose grandmothers spent only two hours fetching wood and fodder now face all-day mountain climbs to carry out the same task.

34

Women as consumer activists

Women in Europe, North America and other industrialized regions are the majority of consumers, shopping for their families' needs as well as their own. Their purchasing choices have potentially tremendous influence over business practices. Here, too, women are initiators of movements that promote consumers' awareness of the environmental impact of various products. Inspired by Rachel Carson's ground-breaking 1962 book, *Silent Spring*, which sounded the first alarm about pesticides, women have taken the lead in alerting buyers to possible dangers in the widespread use of chemical pollutants, toxic sprays and radiation.

In the United Kingdom, the Women's Environment Network led a campaign to educate the public about the environmental and health problems associated with chlorine-bleached paper products; as a result chlorine is no longer used to bleach diapers, tea bags and other products. In the United States, the Women's Environment & Development Organization (WEDO) has organized public hearings with environmental groups and breast cancer victims to focus attention and research funds on links between environmental pollutants and diseases of the reproductive system. The impetus for the coalition effort is the growing epidemic of breast cancer that affects one out of eight women in the U.S. over an 85-year lifespan. Women in other countries are joining the campaign designed to identify environment-cancer links and take preventive measures to protect women's health.

Making connections

The coming of age of the global women's environment movement was spurred by two major United Nations actions. A United Nations commission headed by Norway's ecology-minded prime minister, Gro Harlem Brundtland, issued a ground-breaking study, "Our Common Future", linking the environmental crisis to unsustainable development and financial practices that were worsening North/South inequities, with women a majority of the world's poor and illiterate. And the General Assembly mandated a United Nations Conference on Environment and Development (UNCED), an Earth Summit to be held in Rio de Janeiro, together with a parallel NGO Forum, in June 1992.

In preparation for the Rio conference, two seminal events were held that have since been described as a watershed in addressing the linkages between the global ecological crisis, development inequities, population concerns and the status of women and girls. Sponsored by the UN Environment Programme and organized by WorldWIDE network, the Global Assembly of Women and the Environment in November 1991 brought together in Miami, Florida, more than 200 women who represented environmental "success stories"—grass-roots initiatives that were considered visible, sustainable, affordable and replicable. Their stories demonstrated that women were effective environmental leaders in solving a wide variety of problems in every region of the world.

Immediately following the Assembly, WEDO held the first World Women's Congress for a Healthy Planet, which featured dozens of workshops and a tribunal of five women judges taking testimony from 15 women experts who presented documented analyses of how the environment/development crisis affected and involved women. Attended by 1,500 women from 83 countries, the Congress aimed to bring women's perspectives into the discussions and drafting of UNCED's Agenda 21 and other official documents. Congress participants formulated and unanimously adopted their own agenda, Women's Action Agenda 21, which was presented on the spot to UNCED Secretary-General Maurice Strong, who praised the women's efforts.

The Women's Action Agenda made recommendations on practical steps that could be taken by the United Nations, Governments, industry and NGOs on a host of linked issues, including equality for women in decision-making, democratic rights, militarism and the environment, foreign debt and trade, poverty, land rights and credit for women, population policies and women's health, biodiversity and biotechnology, nuclear power and alternative energy, environmental ethics and use of women's consumer power to protect the environment.

The women's agenda became a unifying force among concerned women's NGOs around the world as they worked together during the United Nations preparatory process leading up to Rio. Broadly representative women's caucuses engaged in the biggest-ever advocacy effort at the UNCED PrepComs, with the result that the final Agenda 21 approved at Rio dedicated an entire chapter to women's roles in sustainable development and also included about 120 other references and recommendations related to women throughout the document.

Toward empowerment

The issues-linkages developed during the UNCED process have produced the most diverse, well-informed, effective and rapidly growing international women's rights movement in history. Based on their experiences with the Earth Summit process, women NGOs have been turning out in record numbers and transforming policy documents approved at subsequent UN conferences at Vienna (human rights), Cairo (population and development), Barbados (small islands) and Copenhagen (social development). All these documents are infused with recognition of women's crucial roles in environment and development.

As a result of women's ongoing organized efforts, the Draft Platform for Action, approved at the 39th session of the United Nations Commission on the Status of Women (15 March–7 April 1995) includes a section devoted to the crucial roles of women in environmental management. It includes important recommendations to the United Nations, Governments, international organizations, the private sector and NGOs to ensure that women are fully involved in environmental/development decision-making and that their priorities and perspectives are reflected in all aspects of decision-making.

By reiterating the need for greater recognition and support for women's concerns, the Platform for Action reminds the world that ensuring the survival and well-being of our planet requires the full empowerment of the female half of humanity.

Women and the environment: success stories

In Russia, Maria Cherkasova, an internationally acclaimed ecologist who specializes in rare and endangered species, believes that nuclear testing, fallout and such disasters as Chernobyl and similar less-publicized accidents are responsible for her country's fast-growing human mortality rates. An increasing number of babies are born with abnormalities and 75% of pregnant women have serious health problems, she says. Her Center for Independent Ecological Programs has created the Suzdal Children's Center, where children with environmental health problems can be rehabilitated in unpolluted surroundings, a project that won her the United Nations Environment Programme's Global 500 award in 1992.

In Japan, when painter Mayumi Oda learned that her Government was importing 1.7 tons of reprocessed plutonium from France—the most toxic radioactive substance on earth—she contacted several Japanese women's groups and they founded the Plutonium-Free Future Women's Network. The group organized international protests that resulted in several Governments denying the plutonium shipments passage through their territorial waters. The network is conducting a worldwide campaign demanding an end to all nuclear weapons and a ban on the production, transportation and reprocessing of plutonium and other nuclear wastes.

In Palau, a tiny island with a population of 15,000 located midway between the Philippines and Indonesia, women have struggled against international pressures for 12 years to uphold a nuclear-free constitution, the only one in the world. Julita Tellei founded the Palau Resource Institute five years ago to convince people that environmental, social and cultural impact assessments must be done before a development project begins. She was among the leaders of the successful effort of Otil a Belaud, a women's and young people's organization, to block Japanese, Iranian and American plans to build a superport oil terminal in Palau. "If we allowed oil tankers and there was an accident", she says, "the entire livelihood of the island—tourism and fishing—would be gone." The superport plans were dropped, and for its work the group received a United Nations Environment Programme Global 500 award in 1993.

In Colombia, Alegria Fonseca, a member of Parliament, conducted an ongoing campaign to stave off tourist development in a coastal reserve rich in wildlife species and habitat. In other Latin American countries women have been instrumental in promoting self-sufficient agriculture, the preservation and use of indigenous plants, and the preservation of rain forests. In Brazil, environmental lawyer Sonia Regina de Burito Pereira is in the forefront of the campaign to preserve the Amazon River. A Venezuelan woman, Alicia Garcia Scarton, was pivotal in opposing a proposed TransAmazon race and car rally that would cut through a pristine wilderness area. Other highly trained women have started successful fish farming projects, fostered organic farming, initiated bans on logging and introduced appropriate technologies.

In Madagascar, where 90 per cent of the original forest has disappeared, Charlotte Rajeriarison initiated an environmental education programme that teaches farmers how to fertilize soil with animal manure as an alternative to burning the forest for nutrients. Children and adults also learn to practice agro-forestry techniques that protect the soil while producing larger harvests. Her efforts earned Ms. Rajeriarison UNEP's Global 500 Award.

Women in the Indonesian mountain village of Bumiredjo responded to recurring diarrhoeal epidemics (due to contaminated water) by initiating a project to secure water from a spring located 500 metres above in a neighbouring village. After negotiating access to the spring with leaders of the other village, they designed and raised funds for a new water system, which it took three years for village men to build.

The system is managed collectively, with women taking turns cleaning the communal water facilities and collecting maintenance fees from each household. As a result of the clean water supply, infant mortality has decreased dramatically and diarrhoea has largely been eliminated. Women are now able to devote more time to income-generating activities. The improved water supply supports agriculture, fish farming and livestock production and has contributed to raising the villagers' incomes and standard of living.

Bella Abzug is a founder and one of the 10 regional co-chairs of the US-based Women's Environment & Development Organization (WEDO).

WORK AND POWER

WOMEN AND ECONOMIC DECISION-MAKING

Women will have to wait at least 450 years before they are represented in equal numbers with men in the higher echelons of economic power. At the current rate of progress, they will reach equality with men in decision-making positions only around the year 2465, reports the United States Fund for a Feminist Majority. A United Nations study puts the date even further away—around the year 2490! Should women wait that long to achieve equality in economic decision-making?

No, they cannot and probably will not. Overwhelming evidence indicates that women are pressing, individually and collectively, to assume positions of power on boards and as managers, in business and banking. They wish to influence the direction of the huge resources controlled by corporations, and have a voice in shaping our future. Women's meaningful participation in strategic decision-making, it is increasingly recognized, is not just good for women but good for organizations, business and society.

These points were among the conclusions of an Expert Group Meeting on Women and Economic Decision-making held in November 1994 in New York. Convened by the United Nations Division for the Advancement of Women (DAW), the meeting was held in preparation for the Fourth World Conference on Women, held in Beijing, China, from 4 to 15 September 1995. Promoting women's full and equal participation in power structures and decision-making at all levels and in all areas is one of the 11 critical areas of concern identified in the Conference's Draft Platform for Action.

Credit is due

Women constitute about half of the world's population. They do about 55 per cent of the world's work when unpaid economic activities in the household are taken into account. This is without even considering unpaid and unrecognized domestic services in households. Yet official statistics report a far lower number of women as "economically active", often ignoring women's economic contributions to the household in agriculture and food processing and other goods production. Domestic services such as child-bearing, child-rearing, cooking and cleaning and family care are rarely recognized as having any economic value at all.

Economic decision-making
At the current rate of progress it would take **475 Years** for women to reach equality with men as senior managers.

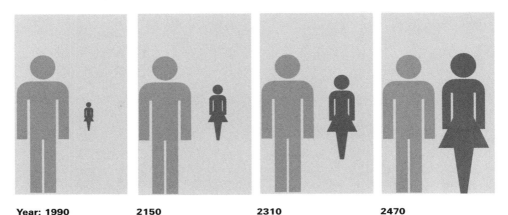

| Year: 1990 | 2150 | 2310 | 2470 |

Source: 1994 World Survey on the Role of Women in Development, United Nations 1995

In India, only 29 per cent of women were reported as economically active in 1990. But when the data were re-analysed to follow the International Labour Organization (ILO) definition of economically active, the figure jumped to over 80 per cent, nearly the same as men, because of women's unrecognized and unpaid economic contributions at home.

Today, more women are working and being paid. According to the 1994 World Survey on the Role of Women in Development, women are entering the formal labour market in unprecedented numbers, at a rate far greater than men. In fact, the Survey notes, the averages show that the ratio of women to men in the economically active population has almost doubled over 20 years.

- *About 854 million women were estimated to be economically active worldwide in 1990, accounting for 32 per cent of the global labour force. Approximately one third (34 per cent) of all women aged 15 years and older are in the labour force.*

Women are also playing an increasingly important role as small-scale entrepreneurs. In the United States, according to a paper presented at the DAW Expert Group Meeting, over 6.5 million enterprises with fewer than 500 employees are owned or controlled by women. In China, one third of the total of 14 million self-employed are women. In Australia, one third of its small and medium-sized enterprises are owned by women and another 28 per cent jointly owned by men and women. In several West African countries and in Haiti, women play a key role in the trading sector as petty traders marketing basic foodstuffs and consumer goods.

- *In Togo and Ghana, the so-called "Mama Benz" women are proving to be a powerful business group. In a world otherwise dominated by men, these women—who own their own Mercedes Benz automobiles, hence the name "Mama Benz"—control much of the national cloth trade. With their counterparts in Zaire, Angola and other countries, these women exercise great influence on the national and cross-boundary trade.*

42

Still not making decisions

- Recently, Jane Royston went to Digital's European headquarters in Geneva, Switzerland, to tell a group of senior managers why they needed her small software company, Natsoft S.A. Created in 1987, her company was earning SF 6.4 million by 1993, an increase of 30 per cent from 1992, and employing 45 people (average age 32 and 25 per cent women). Recognized as the best businesswoman in Switzerland in 1993, she was sufficiently important and successful to keep the senior board members' attention. Most of them, however, were more than attentive: they were transfixed. The 35-year-old woman entrepreneur addressing them was not only brilliant, dynamic and creative, she was also nine months pregnant—and even that fact certainly did not seem to slow her.[1]

Businesswomen like Jane Royston are no longer oddities. More women are now sitting in corporate boardrooms, making policy decisions. But their number as decision makers is still low compared to their number as workers. Globally, less than 20 per cent of managers and 6 per cent or less of senior management are women. The *Review and Appraisal of the Nairobi Forward-looking Strategies* and the 1994 *World Survey on the Role of Women in Development* show that female decision makers are often concentrated in traditional sectors such as education and nursing, but are scarce in top managerial posts at the executive level.

- The proportion of women in top governmental decision-making positions (ministerial level or higher) is relatively low, comprising only 6.2 per cent of all ministerial positions. In economic ministries (including finance, trade, economy and planning ministries and central banks), women's participation is even lower, 3.6 per cent. In 144 countries, no women at all are in these areas and at these levels. However, women's participation in public economic decision-making has increased. In 1987, no women held decision-making posts in economic ministries or central banks in 108 of the 162 Governments studied. By 1994, only 90 Governments out of 186 lacked women in these posts.

- At the corporate level, United States companies have a higher proportion of women managers (8 women for every 100 men) than companies in Asia and Europe (1 woman executive for 100 male executives). Most women managers are concentrated at lower levels of corporate decision-making, with the largest percentage found in the third tier, where 97 per cent and 61.5 per cent of women managers are found for United States and non–United States corporations, respectively.

Why we need more women managers

ILO, which has been at the forefront of international efforts to promote the cause of women workers, notes three reasons why it is important for women to play an equal role in decision-making.

Firstly, it is a question of human rights. Women constitute about half the world's population and more than one third of the workforce. Equality of opportunity and treatment in employment is their right.

Second, it is a matter of social justice. Discrimination against women is at its harshest when it comes to employment.

Third, it is an essential requirement for the acceleration and effectiveness of development, as women are able to contribute their abilities and creativity. They can also ensure a better balance in the allocation of resources and distribution of the benefits of progress.

The obstacles

The 1994 *World Survey on the Role of Women in Development* identifies three factors leading to women's poor representation at the decision-making level, especially in the private sector: a predominantly male culture of management, the continuing current effects of past discrimination, and the lack of recognition of women's actual and potential contribution to economic management.

"Usually, if women gain access to entry-level jobs in large corporations, they tend to remain in the lower ranks and to be concentrated in women-dominated bureaucracies and management organizations. Women's choices tend also to be determined by gender-ascribed roles that thus limit their access to potential career posts", notes the *World Survey*.

What also works against women's professional advancement is the so-called "glass ceiling", an invisible but impassable barrier, formed out of biased work conditions and the male corporate culture. For example, employment rules, regulations and performance evaluation systems tend to be gender-based. "Since conditions of work are largely constructed around the interests of men as employees and employers, they are often unsympathetic towards and unsupportive of the behaviour, roles and outlook of women. Biased attitudes are also embedded in the so-called corporate culture and take forms such as sexual harassment, the exclusion of women from developmental opportunities, the exclusion of women from formal and informal networks and the downgrading of women's skills", notes the *World Survey*.

Other obstacles are more structural. Low levels of literacy and lack of opportunities for training are among them. For women in most developing countries, labour is their single most important resource; yet they often do not have the necessary skills to raise their productivity in both household and market-based production. Their access to productive resources such as capital, technology and land is limited. Though women's right to own land is recognized in many developing countries, their actual control of land is rare. Similarly, custom-bound laws of inheritance, ownership and control of property tend to work against women.

They also have to face situational obstacles such as their family responsibilities as mothers and wives. Strong negative views about women's ability to assume leadership positions add further barriers.

- *In the United States, women's business start-ups fail 7 to 11 per cent more often than men's because of their lack of access to capital, reported the United States National Women's Business Council. In some countries, women need consent from their male relatives before applying for credit. Bankers often ask them to have a male co-signer.*

According to the International Fund for Agricultural Development (IFAD), only 5 per cent of the $5.8 billion in multilateral bank loans allocated to agricultural and rural development in developing countries reached rural women in 1990. In some African countries, women, who account for more than 60 per cent of the agricultural labour force, receive less than 10 per cent of the credit allocated to small farmers and 1 per cent of the total credit allocated to agriculture.

Even when loans are given to women, often they are appropriated by male members of the family. A recent study on loan use in Bangladesh, where several highly successful loan programmes for women are in operation, shows that in only 37 per cent of the cases do women retain full or significant control over loan use. In about 63 per cent of the cases, women have partial, limited or no control.

The "glass ceiling" factor

The term "glass ceiling" was first coined by *The Wall Street Journal* in 1986 to describe the invisible barriers that stand between women and their rise to higher jobs. Though women have done well in the United States—better than women in many other countries—the glass ceilings still remain.

Based on surveys of 4,000 senior executives in the United States, researchers of Stroock & Stroock Lavan recently found it is not efficiency that matters most when considering the promotion of women executives. The combination of factors such as personality, networking ability, loyalty, integrity and political skill is more influential than efficiency alone.

Another study, conducted by the Center for Creative Leadership, found that women were not considered for difficult or international assignments because managers felt women would not be able to cope with the pressure. Women could be fully qualified, but often lost out to men because of such preconceived notions.

Breaking the "entrepreneurial mystique"

Yang Yurong, now 39, was the leader of the production team in charge of women's welfare in a village co-operative in China's Guangxi region. In 1979, she decided to go into business. She borrowed 150 yuan and bought some ducklings and pigs. She also bought books on raising ducks and learned one or two "secret" tricks from her mother on the subject. The first batch of ducks she sold brought her two yuan apiece. With the money earned, she bought more ducklings. As her skill increased, so did her flock. In 1987, a large State-owned duck farm invited her to be a technical adviser. After eight months on the farm, she returned with 1,000 yuan, a wealth of experience and a bold new idea: to build a poultry farm all her own. She decided to raise a special kind of chicken known for its delicious meat but also most vulnerable to disease. She read books, attended lectures and experimented with new medicines. She also raised 100 geese, feeding them on a diet of fermented and cooked duck droppings mixed with vegetables. One year later, Yang's farm earned her more than 10,000 yuan. [2]

At a time when they face new opportunities and continuing risks, women like Yang are increasingly entering the ranks of management. They are overcoming obstacles, often through collective action, but mostly through individual talents and persuasiveness. They are proving that, with adequate training and support, they not only perform well but may be better suited than men to modern management.

Naisbett and Auburdine, authors of *Megatrends 2000*, call the 1990s the Decade of Women in Leadership. The influx of women in the workforce will continue to change the dynamics of the workplace, they underscore. In place of the old, autocratic style of the 1960s and 1970s, corporations with an eye on surviving the present and thriving in the future will encourage entrepreneurial talent irrespective of gender.

The 1994 *World Survey on the Role of Women in Development* is also encouraging, noting indications of dramatic changes in the decades ahead. First, the participation of women in the formal employment market is increasing. Secondly, women are beginning to enter tertiary education in fields like law, business, and science and technology at a faster rate than men. As a result, the pool of entry-level executives will increasingly consist of women. Thirdly, as managerial styles change to become more flexible, women's skills are being recognized as important for business.

Levelling the playing field

Despite obvious progress, women are still handicapped by their unequal access to the essential inputs and policy for entrepreneurial activity. Public action is needed "to level the playing field so that women can compete in the market on the same basis as men". The expert group meeting on women's economic decision-making, in its final report, suggested specific measures to this end:

Transforming financial systems: To succeed as entrepreneurs, women should receive credit in their own right and be able to hold land and other assets.

- *Governments should enact laws to give property rights to women. Finance ministries and central banks should encourage organizational as well as structural changes in financial systems, including reallocation of government and external funds for women entrepreneurs, and encourage setting up small- and micro-enterprise financing.*

- *Commercial banks should recognize the market potential of women in the small- and micro-enterprise sector and structure their services to reach women entrepreneurs.*

Building capabilities and commercial links: to become successful entrepreneurs and managers, women need basic cash- and credit-management skills.

- *Enterprise associations, business NGOs and national training institutes can provide women with training, advisory and monitoring programmes in these areas. Women also need advice on legal rights related to assets, land tenure and credit access.*

- *Women-owned micro-businesses can create collective ventures and forge links with larger women-owned business organizations. International networks of women's organizations should also develop monitoring, joint venture, technical and commercial linkages among women-owned enterprises within regions and globally.*

46

Organizing for economic clout: Women should take action collectively and individually by using their economic power as workers, consumers, voters, managers, executives and entrepreneurs.

- *They can use their vote to increase the number of women in public life. They can create pressure groups at various levels to influence official decision-making.*

- *Women's managerial and entrepreneurial organizations may also forge alliances to raise women's representation in all economic decision-making forums.*

- *Databases should be developed to highlight potential role models in all sectors, including business. Institutions at national and international levels should be committed to developing gender-disaggregated data defining the magnitude of women's economic contribution and the gaps between policies and practices.*

Women themselves must take steps as individuals to get ahead, according to Marion Gétaz, Founder and President of the Women's Institute of Management in Lausanne (Switzerland). "It is up to them to demand the necessary supplementary training and education and to make sure that they are not permanently excluded from career advancement", Ms. Gétaz told ILO's *World of Work* magazine.

Women in Management: lagging behind

Ratio of women to men in administrative and management occupations by region, 1980 and 1990. Number of women per 100 men

Region	1980	1990
Africa	10	18
Asia and the Pacific	9	10
Eastern Europe	30	66
Latin America and the Caribbean	24	34
Western Europe and other	23	41
World	19	34

Source: Division for the Advancement of Women of the United Nations Secretariat, from data contained in the Women's Indicators and Statistics Data Base(WISTAT), version 3, 1994.

1. From a paper presented at DAW Expert Group Meeting, 5-11 November 1994, by Claire L. Bangasser.
2. Story adapted from "Rural Women in China", published by the International Fund for Agricultural Development, Rome, 1994.

MEASURING WOMEN'S UNPAID WORK

It is still before sunrise, about 6:30 a.m., when the researcher arrives at the family's doorstep. For the next hour, as unobtrusively as possible, she records what each household member is doing, at that hour probably washing and getting dressed, preparing breakfast, feeding livestock, gathering materials for school or market. Each separate activity is timed, and all interactions within the household recorded—a mother helping a child or elderly parent with shoes or hair, for instance. For the rest of the day, the researcher will alternate visits at this and another nearby household, observing all activities and interviewing household members about what they did during her absence. To minimize intrusion, no more than four hours are spent with either family in a given day.

The researcher is taking the first painstaking steps in the process of gathering gender statistics. The technique is an old one, a time-use study. The results will be new: when compiled, the data will capture many activities not captured before. Up to now, these activities have been statistically invisible. They are usually not included in conventional data collection, and are therefore largely unvalued—and are mostly undertaken by women. A few examples tell the story: the woman who works as a dressmaker in her spare time who is paid in cash or in kind by her customers, the income unrecorded and the final product uncounted; the older woman who cares for her grandchildren while her daughter is away at work; the farmer's wife who helps plant and harvest the commercial crops, tends the poultry and the kitchen garden completely unassisted and is unpaid. Her role as a housewife, difficult and time-consuming, is not valued in conventional economic terms—and she herself probably thinks of being a housewife as "doing nothing".

The challenge: correcting the database

That informal, unpaid and household production needs to be measured and valued was recognized in principle two decades ago, at the first world conference on women in Mexico City. Despite an avalanche of other computer-generated statistics, there was and still is almost no available data, especially in the developing countries, on the extent and value of what women do. This statistical gap is more than a gender issue: it goes to the heart of effective economic and social policy planning. Statistics, which may appear mind-numbing to many, are, in fact, the engines that drive the decision-making process. It begins with gross domestic product (GDP). If this base figure is wrong or inadequate, so will be all the government functions which follow, such as social services, urban planning, transportation and education.

GDP, a nation's total output of goods and services, tends to omit as much as it includes. In sub-Saharan Africa, for example, women are estimated to be responsible for more than 80 per cent of food production for home consumption, and over half of all agricultural production. Official GDP figures for the region, however, generally count only the produce actually brought to market or exported—the cash crops grown largely by men.

The System of National Accounts (SNA), which determines GDP, was revised to include all goods produced in the household and, by extension, production-related activities like water-carrying. All of the dressmaker's output, part of the so-called informal sector, became recognized economic production. Although unpaid domestic and personal services (cooking, mending, child care etc.) are still not included, the 1993 SNA suggests that alternate concepts of GDP be devised for use in satellite accounts.

Eliminating gender bias

Clearly, part of the problem lies behind the statistics, in methods that are either gender-biased or at best gender-neutral. In censuses and surveys, for example, a resident male is assumed to be the head of household and is usually the one interviewed. Any bias in his response will be recorded as fact, which, in combination with other similar facts, will be used ultimately to determine government policies.

The challenge for the statistician is to develop and implement new concepts and methods of collecting data that will reflect reality and document changes in the situations of both men and women. This can also mean accounting for factors affecting gender to reveal some of the causes of inequalities. A tally of schools, for example, should include the number of female students who "drop out". These statistics can indicate where school schedules might be tailored to fit seasonal work patterns in various geographic areas, to encourage more girls to attend and stay in school. Perhaps most important, accurate baseline data will also help Governments set realistic goals —and more effective policies for achieving them.

Development of valid gender statistics must be a two-pronged process: eliminating gender bias in conventional data collection and filling in the glaring statistical gap in calculating national productivity, i.e., the contribution of women's—and men's— unpaid and household work. Eliminating gender bias in conventional statistics means reviewing and questioning past assumptions and adapting old techniques accordingly. Age and sex are important variables, and the same questions asked of men and women may elicit different responses. Routinely interviewing only male heads of household, for instance, may not indicate the true division of responsibilities among family members or reflect the priorities of the whole family. Similarly, policies designed for heads of household do not necessarily mean improvements for the rest of the family. Gender-specific information should therefore be carefully integrated into all conventional censuses and surveys.

Redefining a day's work

Currently, there is only one comprehensive technique for measuring unpaid work: systematic time-use surveys to demonstrate how a person uses his or her time, provide accurate estimates of unpaid household activities and show the daily, weekly and seasonal patterns of such activities and their relationship to economic and non-economic activities. Such detailed accountings of how days are spent, whether at work, play, eating or sleeping, have been widely used in the industrialized countries but in only a handful of developing nations. The techniques usually required—distribution of diaries and interviews by specially trained personnel—are frequently inappropriate to developing countries, particularly in remote rural areas, where literacy rates tend to be low.

The need for basic data is greatest in precisely these areas, however. In Nepal, for example, although more than two thirds of family income is generated by household-level enterprises, including subsistence agriculture, 1993 GDP figures indicate that much of the post-harvest or later food processing, done primarily by women, is left out; only the production of cottage and other industries is included. This means that GDP omits many minor crops grown—mainly by women—for household consumption.

New techniques being developed by researchers are designed to capture uncounted work as well as the potentially far greater economic contribution of domestic services. All data is separated by gender to reflect the true impact of these activities on both the household's welfare and the national economy as a whole. Statisticians in several countries are currently working to develop a new satellite accounts system to help document and further define the dimensions and productivity of the household economy.

Separate categories would be established to include all unpaid activities done for others, such as cleaning, laundry and handling family finances. The new satellite accounts system would also include "personal development" activities, such as education and skills training, which have important investment value. These would be calculated as part of an extended concept of GDP. Other personal activities, such as eating, sleeping and recreation, which clearly cannot benefit or be performed by anyone else, would be categorized as either personal maintenance (e.g., washing one's own hair as opposed to giving someone else a shampoo) or personal consumption (e.g., reading, watching TV). These would be excluded from the actual accounting of production, but the time spent on them might be measured as a component of the quality of life.

Potential pitfalls

Of course there are some problems in the time-use approach. For example, practically no one engages in any activity in isolation or in strict sequence. Many different tasks and the time spent on them tend to be simultaneous or to overlap. Simultaneous activities are frequent in a household environment, particularly where child care is involved. Rarely does a mother do anything, whether cooking a meal or travelling to visit a friend, that doesn't coincide with some other activity related to child care. These same overlapping activities can cross into the economic area as well, e.g., a mother tending a cash crop with a child at her side.

Next steps

Despite these problems, collection of time-use data remains the only valid method for capturing normally overlooked activities. Development of general methodological guidelines, a combination of conventional statistical theory and field observation, is the necessary next step.

One survey, which included the pre-dawn visit described earlier, used conventional time diaries that were completed using a combination of direct observation and a listing of activities recalled by the subjects during face-to-face interviews. It was designed to document all productive activities undertaken by the men, women and children in 100 households. Five different communities were selected to represent a cross-section of the society at all income levels, in both urban and rural settings. The results were encouraging; the time-use data did in fact reveal many activities not before included in statistics.

Establishing a system of satellite accounts to include unpaid domestic services would estimate the quantity and value of all these statistically "new" activities. In one approach, this means estimating the market value of the labour inputs, which in turn requires carefully measuring the time used. A broad range of possible methods can be used to value non-market production—for example, by determining the number of shirts or dresses a woman could make and sell in the time she spends on child care every day. The time-use study would indicate the amount of time spent; the market price of the hypothetical garments would equal the value of that time.

The impact of a system of satellite accounts could be enormous, helping to provide an accurate accounting of essentially private matters for crucial public purposes. While development policies are generally geared to increasing productivity, increases in productivity are not necessarily reflected in increases or improvements in standards of living. In the industrialized countries, for instance, there are questions about the real benefits of full-time employment for mothers in the absence of adequate child-care arrangements or more sharing of household responsibilities by fathers. In the developing countries, living standards may actually deteriorate while GDP rises. Preliminary studies in Nepal show that, as a result of increased commercialization of farm produce, household members tend to work longer hours, travel farther, spend more on superfluous consumer goods and sometimes even eat less, as more and more home production is sent to market. Economic development, in this case, is an illusion.

Time allocations for paid and unpaid work by sex, 1990-1991, hours per week

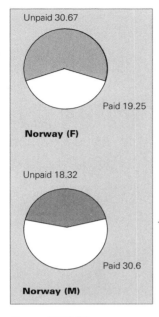

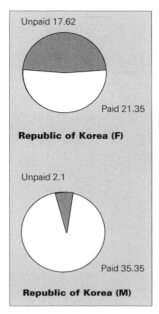

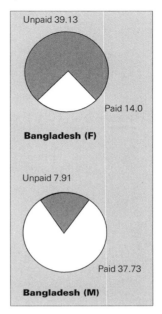

Source: INSTRAW

Inclusion of time-use data and establishing a satellite system of national accounting will dispel the illusions and make clear the magnitude and value of unpaid household work. Perhaps more important, it will show that the burden is carried disproportionately by women, beginning with the fact that they almost invariably work longer hours. In the case of Nepal, time-use data show that women not only match men hour for hour in paid work, but in non-marketable activities they outwork men by two to one.

Equally significant, placing a recognized value on unpaid work will demonstrate a woman's social as well as economic contribution as a provider of a wide range of vital services. This is particularly true in many rural areas, where no services may be available and women have generally provided them without recognition or assistance. With statistical visibility and value, women would be entitled to access to the same services—such as education, health care and sanitation—as the rest of the society.

The next steps inevitably will be a process of trial and error. Any new techniques will require testing, refinement and, to the extent possible, standardization. Finding a statistically valid formula for measuring and evaluating the data collected will require accounting for wide variations in local and national conditions. The procedure will be exacting and tedious, but ultimately it will bring the long-range goal set at Mexico City into reach: the heretofore invisible contributions of women will become visible—accepted, evaluated and integrated into the world's economies.

Written in association with the United Nations International Research and Training Institute for the Advancement of Women (INSTRAW).

53

WOMEN AND INDUSTRY

Jitbarek Hagare was already a rarity—a female graduate of the Department of Mechanical Engineering at the University of Technology in Ethiopia—when she was recruited by the Ethiopian Marble Industry in 1984 to work on a project headed by another woman. In 1985, despite negative attitudes expressed by some of the factory managers, she was sent to Italy for training in marble quarrying and processing technology, and then to Turkey to learn about modern export-oriented marble production and management. Six months later, her skills bolstered by career counselling, exposure to daily operational activities and on-the-job training, she was promoted to the post of Assistant Production Manager. Today Jitbarek Hagare is in charge of four factories, supervising 200 employees, 30 of whom are women.

The aim of sustainable industrial development is to provide people—both men and women—with options for a better future. Through its close links with other productive sectors, particularly agriculture and services, industry opens up job opportunities and provides goods which ultimately improve the quality of life. Any meaningful global agenda for development should recognize the role of people-centred and sustainable industrialization in addressing socio-economic issues. It should also recognize the significant part women play, both as producers and as consumers.

Unfortunately, Jitbarek Hagare's case—a woman from a developing country with a successful career in industry—is still highly unusual. Industry continues to suffer from a gender bias; major adjustments have to be made before women can participate on an equal footing with men in shaping the structure of industrial development so that economic benefits can be balanced with social progress.

Women: one third of the manufacturing labour force

The word "industry" conjures up images of sweaty men, deafening machines and smokestacks. Although it is true that most heavy industries are still dominated by men, studies carried out by the United Nations Industrial Development Organization (UNIDO) since 1992 confirm that on a global average, women account for a third of the manufacturing labour force. If one were to include the invisible brigades of home-based women producing goods through sub-contracting arrangements, the number would probably rise to 40 per cent. Add to this the countless women who work at the bottom end of the market as operators of small-scale and micro-enterprises, producing low-cost goods and processed foods, and the number could rise to 60 per cent. In countries where industrialization has been both swift and successful, the participation of women in manufacturing has been even more significant, particularly in the lowest salary and occupational groups. This is particularly true in the case of export-oriented economies.

The greater proportion of the female workforce is found in micro- to medium-sized industries, in both the formal and informal sectors, as well as in export-oriented industries, where women make a valuable contribution to the overall socio-economic development of society. A more detailed and accurate assessment of the number of women involved is hampered by a conspicuous lack of statistical data on the productive activities carried out by women in the non-structured sectors of the economy as well as in various sub-sectors of industry.

There is a positive relationship between social development indicators and women's participation in manufacturing. As women take on salaried jobs in the manufacturing sector, there is a corresponding increase in literacy, improvement in life expectancy and lowering of fertility rates, all helping to break the circle of poverty and enhance the empowerment of women. Therefore, any policy measures relating to industrial development must take into account the crucial contribution of the female industrial workforce to economic, industrial and social progress.

What are the obstacles?

International trends: In times of economic hardship, women are still most likely to feel the crunch. Particularly in developing and industrializing countries, global restructuring, trade-liberalization policies and the relocation of manufacturing industries all conspire to limit women's opportunities and force them to take up productive activities as entrepreneurs or to enter the workforce in low-skilled jobs in, for example, export-oriented industries.

Education: The continuing disparity between men and women in second- and third-level education, in addition to the existing male bias in employment rates across the regions, makes it difficult and sometimes impossible for women to enter the industrial labour force at other than the lowest-paid, and lowest-skilled, levels. In some countries of Central and Eastern Europe, though more than half the girls entering secondary school opt for a technical track, statistics show they do not go on to have the same career opportunities as men. One reason is undoubtedly that they have far less access to further training and skills upgrading.

Lack of access to credit, training, information and technology: While restricted access to both credit and markets features high on the list of obstacles faced by women entrepreneurs, an Expert Group Meeting on Women in the Food Processing Sector in Africa, organized by UNIDO in January 1994, considered that other constraints deserved equal attention, namely access to information, technologies and training as prerequisites for success.

Stereotypes: Gender stereotypes and cultural, religious and traditional barriers aggravate the situation even further.

These factors and the working conditions experienced by women in industry leave a lot to be desired. Many women are put off by the idea of working in industry due to the absence of child-care and medical facilities at the workplace, the unsafe or unhealthy working conditions and the discrimination they suffer *vis-à-vis* their male colleagues in terms of promotion and training.

The question therefore is not simply whether there should be an increased number of women working in manufacturing, but rather how to address the problems and needs of women who are employed in manufacturing or productive activities as entrepreneurs. Women should be empowered to be equal partners with men in industrial development, whether as technicians, workers, managers or entrepreneurs. Training in both management and technical fields, career counselling and confidence-building for women, alongside gender-awareness training for male co-workers and supervisors, should be instrumental in overcoming these obstacles.

Is the industry responding to the needs of women and the community?

People-centred and sustainable industrial development can go a long way towards creating better living conditions for both women and men.

- *Facet Andina, a non-governmental organization, and UNIDO modernized the centuries-old craft of pottery in the Bolivian village of Huayculi, 9,000 feet up in the Andes. The project specifically targeted women potters, and it achieved significant results. With the construction of a gas-fired kiln for the community, the village infrastructure was improved and productivity increased. Through the introduction of new technologies, a number of back-breaking tasks were eliminated. The installation of the gas-fired kiln, for example, not only relieved women of the chore of fetching firewood for the individual small kilns, but also halted the devestation of vegetation. The subsequent increase in income levels resulted in a reverse-migration trend, and the cultural heritage of one of the Americas' oldest ethnic minorities was preserved.*

Protecting the environment

The Rio Declaration, adopted at the United Nations Conference on Environment and Development (UNCED), recognized the vital role women play in environmental management and development and described their full participation as "essential to achieve sustainable development".

Women are among those who stand to gain from cleaner industrial production technologies. On the one hand, those technologies help combat pollution and promote a better and healthier environment in which women can work and live. On the other hand,

57

technological advances make it possible and affordable for women entrepreneurs to benefit from low-cost, energy-saving techniques beneficial to both their health and the environment.

- *Rural women in the town of Azara in Plateau State, Nigeria, were introduced to solar evaporation techniques for the production of salt, which eliminated the need for fuel wood. The installation of a diesel-fuelled pump relieved women of the arduous task of making 20 or 30 trips to the salt fields each morning, carrying the salt on their heads in heavy pots.*

Towards sustainable solutions

Conventions 100 and 111 of the International Labour Organization (ILO) provide a framework for the legal protection of women in the workplace. Enforcement measures and other actions are still needed if women are to be considered and recognized as equal partners in the economic development of their respective societies.

According to UNIDO, the main challenge is to prepare women to become an integral part of the human-resource base for industrial development, in order to meet the changing requirements of the manufacturing sector. Any strategy for achieving this objective must involve both the private and public sectors.

Technology: the growing challenge

The constant upgrading of technology has been an integral part of the process of industrialization. While introducing new technology may benefit some women in the short and possibly in the long run, observes the 1994 UN report on the Role of Women in Development, in the medium term it displaces women workers in favour of men. Women are disproportionately vulnerable to the impact of technological change because of their concentration in lower-skilled, labour-intensive jobs in both industry and services.

- In the manufacturing sector, the introduction of new technology seems to impact on women in two ways. In cases where rationalization and the reduction of labour-intensive work are the primary goals, women workers suffer as a result of lay-offs. But in cases where productivity improvements are the motivating factor, women often benefit from the consequent regeneration of the enterprise or industry.

- New technology demands new skills, often causing female workers to be displaced in favour of males. However, there are exceptions. With the introduction of electronic data entry, for example, female workers have often displaced male compositors.

The World Survey on Women in Development also sheds new light on the quantitative impact of advance information technology for women in service industries, where they are to a large extent still concentrated in routine occupations most susceptible to rationalization—clerical, bookkeeping, secretarial, typing, cashiers and sales. In the developing world, according to the Survey, women have been the main beneficiaries of employment creation in clerical and data-base entry work. This trend runs counter to a trend in the advanced economies away from clerical and secretarial work towards technical, professional and managerial employment, where women are less likely to be found. The Survey notes that the trends towards increasing employment in clerical and data-entry work in developing countries could therefore be associated as much with the displacement of these jobs in industralized countries (made possible by tele-working or remote working) as with a lag in the introduction of information technology in developing countries.

The wider application of information technology in the service industries creates atypical patterns of employment. Information technology, the World Survey notes, is contributing to a new dualism between a core workforce that is highly trained, multi-skilled and adaptable and a peripheral group of workers whose services can be acquired or dispensed with in response to the needs of the moment. For example, locating telework or data processing outside the mainstream of organization structures lends itself to such dualism, and there have been reports of isolation, minimal job and income security and the disintegration of the collective work ethic.

Prospects and challenges for women by region

Africa	Agriculture plays a more important role than industry. The manufacturing sector is characterized by labour-intensive light industries as well as informal productive activities. Women are only marginally involved in manufacturing and are seriously affected by poverty. Many countries are undergoing industrial restructuring.	**Actions to be taken:** • strengthening of mutual support networks at the community level; • new mechanisms of credit for women entrepreneurs in the formal and informal sectors; • capacity-building programmes to reduce barriers to occupational mobility; • technical assistance including technical skills, management and marketing, linked to credit.
Asia	In many countries, female employment in the manufacturing and service sectors has grown faster than male employment. The majority of women are at the lower end of the occupational scale, in unskilled jobs with few opportunities for career development. A large portion of productive activities of women remain unrecorded.	**Actions to be taken:** • developing methods to collect gender-disaggregated data on the role of women in manufacturing; • changing the public image of non-traditional female roles and occupations in industry; • providing access to women for training in line with the emerging needs of the industrial sector; • reducing gender imbalances in technical education and training.
Europe, USA, Canada	Although the participation rate of women in the manufacturing sector is lower than in the service sector, it is still the highest among the regions, with the greatest concentration of women in the manufacturing sectors of Eastern and Central European countries.	**Action to be taken:** • economically justifiable job creation; in the future, more labour opportunities will depend on innovation in the manufacturing sector, the expansion of services in relation to manufacturing and growth of tertiary activities.
Latin America	A third of the region's labour force is female, employed predominantly in service-sector unskilled jobs in urban areas. Women's participation rate in manufacturing has stabilized at around 16 per cent.	**Actions to be taken:** • improve working conditions for women; • diversify women's participation in various occupational catagories through training and retraining; • assimilate female unemployment caused by privatization; • integrate women in the export and modern service sectors.

The role of UNIDO

Since its inception in 1986 as a specialized agency of the UN system, UNIDO has accorded high priority to the integration of women in industrial development. In the 1990s, "Women in industry" has become a cross-sectoral theme for all UNIDO activities, with a three-pronged approach: a) mainstreaming with a gender perspective; b) a women's component in a large project; and c) women-specific projects to address specific constraints and needs of women.

Particular importance is being attached to enhancing the competitiveness of small-scale industries. For example, UNIDO's comprehensive training programmes in food processing in Africa and Central America upgrade entrepreneurial and marketing skills of women. A thematic programme to upgrade the technical, managerial and marketing skills of existing women entrepreneurs is being successfully applied in selected subsectors and countries in Africa. Similar UNIDO programmes are also being developed or implemented in other regions.

• In Nepal, UNIDO is assisting a women's cooperative enterprise with technology transfer and adaptation, quality control, and marketing of handicrafts and processed food products.

Participation rate of women in manufacturing employment for selected countries

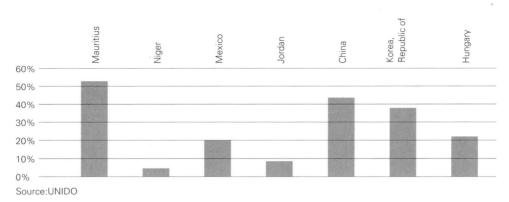

Source: UNIDO

Studies carried out by UNIDO on the role of women in manufacturing have identified several areas for action, adapted to the special needs and constraints of women in various regions of the world.

- In China, a special programme for women entrepreneurs has been developed for the integration of women in the modernization process. When suitably modified and adjusted to local conditions, this programme can be replicated in other countries with economies in transition.

- In sub-Saharan Africa, a joint UNIDO-IFAD project addresses the development and transfer of appropriate technology for rural women. A platform with a multifunctional engine has been put into use for milling and power generation. Apart from adding value to the agricultural products of women, it has also become a source of additional off-season income.

Written in association with UNIDO.

WOMEN AND THE MEDIA

By Margaret Gallagher

"For full eight years I was the only woman on the reporting staff of the great national daily (The Times of India).When I was expecting my first baby and wanted to take maternity leave I was told the rule books had to be consulted, for the Times had no tradition of maternity leave."

Usha Rai, The Times of India, 28 October 1988

"The world's war zones today are chock-a-block with would-be Kate Adie's risking their lives for minor stations in the hope of landing the big story because they know that what the major networks want is a front line account from a (preferably pretty) woman in a flakjacket."

Peter Millar, The Times (of London), 21 August 1992

Usha Rai joined *The Times of India* in the 1960s. Today over 20 per cent of journalists on the *Times* are women. The female reporter is no longer an oddity. In most countries it is now considered unnecessary, or inappropriate, to "protect" women journalists from the crime beat or from night duty. On the contrary, even war zones are no longer forbidden territory to women media professionals. Britain's Kate Adie is just one of many celebrated female journalists seen regularly on television screens around the world, filing courageous stories from the most dangerous trouble spots on earth.Yet the London *Times* suggests that the media somehow manipulate these women. According to this view, the "female personality reporter"—like the female news-reader and the female presenter—is part of a deliberately-thought-out media strategy to attract viewers and readers. Whether this is true or not, it is an indisputable fact that almost everywhere women's share of media jobs has increased steadily over the past two decades, and that female senior executives are not uncommon. But despite these advances, however competent they are, however ready to "risk their lives" in the pursuit of their profession, women working in the media may still be reduced to the status of "a (preferably pretty) woman in a flakjacket". Even today women media professionals are likely to be judged in a quite different way from their male peers.

Of course, this tendency to apply different criteria to women and men permeates media content itself. After 25 years of research into gender portrayal on television in the United States, the Cultural Indicators at the Annenberg School of Communication, University of Pennsylvania, concluded in 1994 that the world depicted by television "seems to be frozen in a time-warp of obsolete and damaging representations ... A child growing up with children's major network television will see about 123 characters each Saturday morning, but rarely, if ever, a role model of a mature female as leader." In the world as seen through the lens of the media, social and occupational roles are almost completely divided along gender lines. When women appear at all—and numerous studies around the world document their dramatic underrepresentation in almost all kinds of media content—they tend to be depicted within the home and are rarely portrayed as rational, active or decisive. Of course there are exceptions. But they remain exceptions. The evidence is overwhelming, whatever part of the world one looks at. The most extensive cross-national study so far, spanning 25 television channels in 10 European countries, found that from one country to another there are "few grounds for optimism. Instead we come across the same dreary litany, an endless repetition of the same statistics, tinged with despair." But why does all this matter?

Why the media matter

The mass media occupy an increasingly central place in the lives of women and men all over the world. If North America, Western Europe and some of the affluent Asian and Arab States still lead in terms of media availability, the global picture is changing fast. Between 1970 and 1991 the developing regions increased their share of world radio sets from 16 per cent to 36 per cent, and their share of world television sets from 8 per cent to 29 per cent, the fastest growth rates being in Africa, the Arab States and Asia.

In many countries of the Caribbean, Latin America and the Pacific, ownership of radio and television sets is already well above the world average. The electronic media are sweeping aside the barriers of illiteracy which have traditionally excluded vast populations from access to information and entertainment via the printed word. People now spend at least 4 hours a day watching television in—for example—the USA, Japan and Portugal. In other countries daily viewing averages of between 2 and 4 hours are common.

The media are well placed to influence our opinions and attitudes—about ourselves, our relationships, our place in the world. But what we see and hear in the media is a selection—reflecting particular priorities and views of the world. That selection—and its presentation in specific media output—reproduces certain assumptions about women's role and status.

Women are enthusiastic media users, and their media preferences are different from those of men. A recent UNESCO study of television viewing patterns found an identical pattern across all nine countries surveyed. Women in Australia, Bulgaria, Hungary,

India, Italy, Korea, the Netherlands, the Philippines and Sweden spend on average 12 per cent more time watching television than men. And while men prefer sports, action-oriented programmes and information (especially news), women prefer popular drama, music/dance and other entertainment programmes. This pattern of preferences mirrors the way women and men are portrayed in various kinds of media: each sex tends to favour media content which gives visibility to their own gender—either in terms of the characters presented or in terms of the issues highlighted.

However, in overall terms women are much less visible in the media than men are. Not surprisingly then, research shows that many women are not satisfied with what the media offer. A 1994 study in the United Kingdom showed that although women feel ambivalent about the concept of "women's issues"—fearing that this kind of labelling will lead to marginalization—there is also a shared understanding among women about issues which do concern them, and a feeling that these are not given priority in the news media. As one woman put it, "Women's issues don't always get enough airtime on the so-called serious programmes. They don't have the same weight as world politics, which they should do, because they are about changing society in fundamental ways."

Most of the women interviewed in this study also said they would like to see more women journalists on television, and more female experts, because these would "act as significant role models for other women, stimulate female interest in public issues, and—perhaps—sometimes speak in the interests of and for women." As these women clearly recognize, access to the media bestows power. Those who produce media content can decide what information and images appear in the media, and also how these are presented. But how easy is it for women to reach these positions?

The media employment gap

UNESCO data show that women have pursued higher-level mass communication education in increasing numbers over the past 15 years. Almost everywhere the percentage of women studying in this area is on the rise. Data covering 81 countries show that in 50 of them more than 50 per cent of journalism and communication students are female. Yet women are still a minority presence within media organizations—whether radio and television or the printed press. Studies conducted in 1993-1994 in selected countries in Africa, Asia, Europe and Latin America show that in no country does women's share of media jobs reach 50 per cent. Indeed, in the majority of cases outside Europe it is well below 30 per cent. The proportion of women finding employment in the mass media is by no means commensurate with their training.

A six-country study coordinated by the Asian Mass Communication Research and Information Centre (AMIC) notes that in all of these countries there is a gap between the number of women who receive communication training and the number working in the media. Studies in the United States and the Netherlands have shown that female journalism graduates are less likely than their male counterparts to find work in journalism.

Of those women who are hired by media organizations, most are actually to be found in administrative jobs rather than in the production and editorial posts usually associated with the creation and development of media output. In almost every country studied in Africa, Asia, Europe and Latin America, more than 50 per cent of all female media workers are found in administration and service jobs. And within the administrative hierarchy, women tend to be concentrated in low-level secretarial and junior management posts.

On the other hand, women are almost invisible in the technical area—where many jobs are highly skilled and highly paid, sometimes leading to careers in programme production or to the senior management echelons. Averaging 8 per cent across the European countries, 5 per cent in Africa and 4 per cent in Latin America, women's poor representation in technical jobs in the media is often attributed to lack of relevant training.

However, this is not the whole story. European research shows that the number of women recruited to the technical area is disproportionately low, even when they have the necessary formal qualifications.

At the heart of the media lie the editorial and production jobs most directly concerned with·the creation of media output. Print journalism offers comparatively good prospects to women, especially in Latin America. Across the six countries studied women are 28 per cent of reporters and "standard" journalists, 29 per cent of correspondents, 36 per cent of sub-editors, 24 per cent of editors, and 21 per cent of bureau chiefs, directors and executive editors. By contrast, there are no women in the bureau chief category in any of the African countries, Japan or Malaysia; in India (across three major dailies) there is just one. In radio and television production there is considerable gender segregation, with women tending to be concentrated in occupations (announcers, presenters, production assistants) which—even if sometimes well-paid—may not lead to onward career development.

However, in most of the countries studied women do have reasonable access to the producer role—33 per cent in Europe, 34 per cent in Africa, 41 per cent in Latin America. In Malaysia 36 per cent of producers are women, and in Indian television the figure is 30 per cent—an extremely high proportion in relation to women's overall share of television jobs (15 per cent). The nature of the producer's role varies considerably from one organization to another, but in many cases it does carry considerable influence. However, among the most influential production executives—heads of department, programme controllers—women's share of posts drops to 16 per cent across the organizations in Latin America, 15 per cent in Europe, 12 per cent in Africa, and 4 per cent in India, while there are no women at all at this level inJapan, Malaysia, Malawi, Namibia or Swaziland.

64

Real power within the media remains largely a male monopoly. Out of more than 200 organizations studied in 30 countries across four regions, only 7 are headed by women; a further 7 have female deputy directors. Most of these are small radio companies or news magazines. In fact women's share of top jobs in the media is still disproportionately small. For example, analysis of the European broadcasting data shows that men are seven times more likely than women to reach the highest positions. As in other fields of employment, the media open their doors more readily to women in the middle echelons than at the very top: the "glass ceiling" is extremely difficult to crack.

Today, although blatant discriminatory practices have generally been abolished, women's access to media power continues to be hindered by a series of "invisible barriers"—attitudes, working conditions, work assignments and so on—which can impede career development in subtle ways. For instance, media organizations generally subscribe to legislative requirements governing equal pay. But ILO data stretching back to 1985 demonstrate a notable earnings gap between female and male journalists—a gap which is actually widening in countries as diverse as Australia, Sweden, the United Kingdom, the Republic of Korea and Singapore, and which is not explained by any difference in the hours worked by these women and men.

The explanation must be sought in more subjective factors such as the relative bargaining power of female and male journalists, the perceived value of their work, and their access to various kinds of assignment.

Women in media: making a difference

Women must still struggle to achieve recognition and respect as media professionals. But the struggle is a crucial one. For the assumption that media content will change for the better if more women are involved in its production has been an integral part of the debate surrounding gender portrayal in the media over the past twenty years. Links between women's employment in the media and changes in the nature of media output are notoriously difficult to demonstrate, and some studies have concluded that female and male media professionals do not necessarily differ in their approaches to stories or issues. Without dwelling on the many reasons why it is difficult for women to change long-established media practices and routines, it is worth noting the comment of Kay Mills, veteran American journalist: "A story conference changes when half the participants are female ...There is indeed security in numbers. Women become more willing to speak up in page-one meetings about a story they know concerns many readers."

The importance of "critical mass" is paramount. Women are still far from being "half the participants" in the media, particularly in key editorial areas. But clearly the numbers are growing—and not just among "rank and file" employees. There is no doubt that in the past few years women have begun to break through to the very top ranks of media organizations, to an extent which would have been unimaginable just a decade ago. And evidence is beginning to emerge that—when they constitute a reasonable numerical force—women can and do make a difference, even in the hallowed area of news. For instance, a 1992 survey of managing editors of the 100 largest daily newspapers in the USA found that 84 per cent of responding editors agreed that women have made a difference—both in defining the news and in expanding the range of topics considered newsworthy: women's health, family and child care, sexual harassment and discrimination, rape and battering, homeless mothers, quality of life and other social issues.

The introduction of "new topics" (although of course they are age-old concerns for women) is one way women media professionals can make a difference. Another is to change the way established issues are covered. To illustrate this, let us return to the world's war zones. It was in one of these—in the former Yugoslavia—that women journalists succeeded in focusing world attention on the systematic rape of women as a weapon of war. Penny Marshall was one of the first British journalists to investigate conditions in the camps at Omarska and Trnopolje—before the issue of mass rape became public. Her remarks are revealing:

*"As soon as I saw the men (in the camps), partly because of their physical appearance, I wanted to know if they had been tortured. It didn't strike me that the women's story was as urgent as the men's, and I think that is because I had inherited a news agenda that has subsequently changed. It has occurred to me since that the next generation of reporters may well put rape on the agenda much higher, and much earlier in the war, **because of this experience**".*

Women's employment in the media: 1993-1994
Percentage of female staff in radio, television and the press

	Radio/TV	Press		Radio/TV	Press
Africa			**Europe**[6]		
Botswana	46.5[1]	32.6[2]	Belgium	31.3	21.5
Lesotho	39.5	35.0[3]	Denmark	42.6	28.9
Malawi	11.4	17.2	France	36.6	—
Mozambique	16.3[4]	—	Germany	38.8[7]	3.0
Namibia	25.0	46.6	Greece	36.3	—
Swaziland	29.8	28.4	Ireland	32.7	—
Tanzania	—	19.0	Italy	30.1	21.0
Zambia	25.2	21.0	Luxembourg	28.6[5]	37.1
Zimbabwe	22.3	18.6	Netherlands	32.8	31.9
Latin America			Portugal	34.1	20.3
Chile	23.0	24.8	Spain	30.2	25.7
Colombia	32.0[5]	30.4	United Kingdom	39.8	24.7
Ecuador	25.4	31.7	**Asia**		
Mexico	23.5	19.4	India	12.2[8]	7.9
Peru	29.0[4]	15.3	Japan	9.0	6.8[9]
Venezuela	24.1	27.4	Malaysia	27.7	25.5

Source: Data based on studies for the Statistical Division of the United Nations Secretariat

[1] Ministry of Information and Broadcasting: includes Radio Botswana, Daily News, Botswana Press Agency; there is no television in Botswana

[2] Weekly press only; see note 1

[3] Lesotho Weekly only; there is no daily press in Lesotho

[4] Radio only

[5] TV only

[6] Radio/TV data for 1990. Press data only permanent staff

[7] Former Federal Republic only

[8] Includes All India Radio (total staff) and Doordarshan TV (headquarters and 7 production centres only)

[9] Excludes temporary staff

Women do "inherit" agendas within the media. But they can also change those agendas, to reflect more adequately the preoccupations and priorities of all women. That is why the media matter.

Women in the media: a sampling of success stories

Eugenia Apostol	(Philippines) Founder and Publisher Philippine Daily Enquirer (1985-1993), launched as an alternative to the government-controlled press of the 1980s and now one of the top circulation dailies in the Philippines
Charlotte Beers	(United States) Since 1992 Chairperson and Chief Executive Officer Ogilvie & Mather Worldwide, one of the world's largest advertising agencies; also first woman to chair the American Association of Advertising Agencies (in 1988)
Leyla Beketova	(Kazakhstan) In 1994 became President of the Kazakhstan Radio and Television Corporation, the country's newly created national broadcasting network
Razia Bhatti	(Pakistan) Chief Executive Newsline Publications and Editor Newsline since its launch in 1989; the award-winning Newsline is one of Pakistan's leading news magazines and is among the few journalist-run publications in South Asia
Danièle Boni Claverie	(Côte d'Ivoire) Has held several top-level posts in the media, including that of Director-General of the national television organization, TV-Ivoirienne (1987-1990), and since 1993 has been her country's Minister of Communication
Tina Brown	(United Kingdom) In 1992 became Editor of The New Yorker, one of America's most prestigious magazines, and also the first magazine editor to receive the National Press Foundation's Editor of the Year award
Man-Yee Cheung	(Hong Kong) Director-General Radio Television Hong Kong since 1986, was the first woman to become President of the Commonwealth Broadcasting Association (1988-1992)
Anne Deveson	(Australia) Executive Director Australian Film, Television and Radio School (1985-1989), was the first woman to be appointed to this position; since 1991 she has chaired Australia's National Working Party on Portrayal of Women in Media
Miriam Fliman	(Chile) Director-General and General Manager Radio Nacional since 1991, is one of the most highly placed women in broadcasting management in Latin America
Ernestina Herrera de Noble	(Argentina) Since 1969 Director El Clarin, Argentina's largest circulation daily, is one of several women now running major newspapers in Latin America
Flor Hurtado	(Mexico) Director-General Canal 11 since 1994, runs Mexico's most important cultural television channel
Jean Kaoka Kalisilira	(Zambia) Acting Editor-In-Chief Zambia News Agency since 1994, is the highest-ranking woman in news agency management in Southern Africa

Janet Karim   (Malawi) Since 1993 Director and Editor-In-Chief The Independent, Malawi's first
independent newspaper, published bi-weekly

Sandra Knowles   (Bahamas) General Manager Broadcasting Corporation of the Bahamas since 1993,
is one of several women now heading broadcasting services in the Caribbean

Gwen Lister   (Namibia) Editor The Namibian, one of Namibia's most influential dailies,
which she launched in 1985; also Chairperson Media Institute of Southern Africa, founded
in 1992 to promote a free and pluralistic press in Southern Africa

Monica Miller   (Samoa) President Pacific Islands News Association since 1991, is the first woman
to head PINA—the largest professional media body in the Pacific region

Pilar Miro   (Spain) Director General Radio Televisión Española (1986-1989) and award-winning
film director, was the first woman to head a major broadcasting organization in
western Europe

Jane Moilanen   (Finland) Managing Director Liikemainonta-McCann (McCann-Erikson Worldwide-
Finland) since 1995, is among the highest-ranking women in European advertising

Christine Ockrent   (France) Since 1994 Editorial Director L'Express, one of France's most significant
weekly news magazines, while continuing a highly successful career in television journalism

Joan Pennefather   (Canada) Chairperson National Film Board of Canada since 1989, heads one of Canada's
most important communication agencies, which has done much to promote women's access
to the media

Ana Maria
Romero de Campero   (Bolivia) Since 1989 Editor-In-Chief Presencia, one of Bolivia's most influential
dailies; so far her country's only female Minister of Information (in 1979), she is
also Vice President International Federation of Daily and Periodical Publications

Lucie Salhany   (United States) Chairperson Fox Broadcasting Company 1993-1994, was the first
woman to rise to the highest echelon of broadcast management in the United States

Batatu Tafa   (Botswana) Deputy Director Broadcasting Radio Botswana since 1990, is one of the
most highly placed women in broadcast management in the African continent

Beverley Wakem   (New Zealand) Director-General Radio New Zealand (1984-1991), maintains the
record of highest-ranking woman in broadcasting management in New Zealand and was the
first female President of the Asia-Pacific Broadcasting Union (1989-1991)

Nancy Woodhull   (United States) Founding Editor USA Today (Circulation almost 2 million)
and its first Managing Editor, was until 1990 President Gannett News Services, one of
America's largest news organizations

LITERACY: A KEY TO WOMEN'S EMPOWERMENT

The young girl, a fifth grader, says goodbye to her classmates. Her mother died recently and she now has to stay home to cook and bring lunch to her father in the field where he works. At home, her grandmother, who is very old and blind, chides her son for withdrawing his daughter from school. "I will cook", she says. "But how can you? You are blind", he says. "What I can see being blind, you cannot see with your eyes open", the old woman replies.

The message of this dramatized public service announcement, broadcast frequently on national television in Bangladesh, is clear. Bangladesh, like many other countries, is opening its eyes to the reality that with almost two thirds of its female population illiterate, national development is severely hampered.

Over the past 30 years, an "education avalanche" has been sweeping across much of the world. Overall, student enrolment has increased, spending on basic education has grown, national and international actions have been taken to raise literacy rates. In most developed regions and in a growing number of developing countries, near universal literacy for young people has been achieved.

Women, too, have benefited from this "quiet revolution". Today, more girls and women are entering school. In some countries, such as Qatar, Dominica and Lesotho, even more women than men are enrolled in higher education.

Despite this progress, years of neglect have left high illiteracy rates among adult, especially rural, women in most developing countries. Huge gaps also exist in women's educational achievements. Women and girls in both developed and developing countries still do not have equal access to education and training resources.

Cold statistics, hard facts

Poor, overworked and illiterate—this is the profile of most adult, rural women in the majority of developing countries. Although they are largely responsible for the health and welfare of family members and in many societies grow a good part of the country's food, these women are often deprived of the very means to perform these functions more efficiently. They can neither read nor write.

According to the 1993 World Education Report of the United Nations Educational, Scientific and Cultural Organization (UNESCO), 905 million men and women—almost a quarter of the world's adult population—are illiterate. About 587 million, or 65 per cent of them, are women. In 1985, the number of illiterate women and men was 592 million and 352 million respectively.

There is also some good news. According to a recent study by the Population Action Council, a U.S.-based study group, of roughly 885 million children going to school in 1993, about 400 million are girls. In some countries, especially in developed ones and some parts of Latin America and the Caribbean, there is already no significant gender gap in education at the primary level. The only regions where male/female disparities remain pronounced are South Asia, the Arab States and Sub-Saharan Africa.

- In much of South Asia and the Middle East, only one student in three is a woman. In Africa less than one primary or secondary student in three, and less than one tertiary student in five, is female.

- In some South Asian and African countries, the illiteracy rate for adult women is over 80 per cent. According to the UN's *The World's Women: Trends and Statistics 1970-1990*, among women aged 30 years and above, illiteracy rates are 93.4 per cent in Nepal, 89.2 per cent in Pakistan, 98.2 per cent in Burkina Faso, 97.9 per cent in Mali and 90.4 per cent in Togo.

- Illiteracy in rural areas continues to be high in most regions, even in countries where urban women have made significant progress. According to *The World's Women*, this is sharpest in Latin America—where the rural illiteracy rate among women aged 15-24 is 25 per cent, compared with 5 per cent in urban areas. In Asia and the Pacific, rural rates are double urban rates (43 per cent compared with 22 per cent), and in Africa three quarters of rural women aged 15-24 are illiterate, compared with less than half in urban areas.

- The drop-out rate among girls is much higher than among boys. In Mali, a recent study found that 80 per cent of girls have never attended any school and 60 per cent of those who have attended dropped out during primary school. In Brazil, only 63 per cent of children who start primary school reach second grade, and only 47 per cent make it to fourth grade.

Favouring education for boys over girls is not exclusively a "third world matter". In developed countries, the ratio of boys and girls going to school is roughly the same at the primary and secondary levels when education is compulsory. But at the tertiary level, boys easily outnumber girls. Similarly, women's access to scientific and technical areas remains limited.

- According to the *Human Development Report 1993*, published by the United Nations Development Programme (UNDP), the ratio of female to male third-level students in scientific and technical fields in Spain is 28 per cent, in Austria 25 per cent and in Canada 29 per cent.

- In the U.S., according to a recent study by the American Association of University Women, girls are systematically excluded from equal education through stereotyping and prejudice. Boys are preferred over girls in subjects such as math, science and technology.

Education: A critical area of concern

According to Mrs. Gertrude Mongella, Secretary-General of the United Nations Fourth World Conference on Women, though there has been broad progress towards universal literacy, a huge historical deficit remains among today's adult women, especially rural women, which denies them full partnership in society.

If women are to contribute effectively to national development into the twenty-first century, "the fundamental question is whether they will be sufficiently equipped to participate fully by receiving a quality education that will prepare them to enter any field, expose them to science, technology and communications and stimulate their creativity", said Mrs. Mongella.

Education was an indispensable objective for two United Nations conferences—the International Conference on Population and Development (September 1994, Cairo, Egypt) and the World Summit for Social Development (March 1995, Copenhagen, Denmark).

Since 1975, when the first World Conference on Women was held in Mexico City, education for women has remained a key issue on the international agenda. The Forward-looking Strategies for the Advancement of Women to the Year 2000, adopted at the third World Conference on Women in Nairobi in 1985, described education as the basis for the full promotion and improvement of the status of women, a basic tool that should be given to women in order to fulfil their role as full members of the society.

In 1990, when the world observed International Literacy Year, the question of equal access to education by women was widely discussed. The same year, the World Conference on Education for All was held in Jomtien, Thailand. The Conference designated education for girls as a top priority. Co-sponsored by UNESCO, the UN Development Programme (UNDP), the UN Children's Fund (UNICEF) and the World Bank, the Conference initiated a number of programmes aimed at reducing the disparity in illiteracy rate between the sexes and eliminating the social and cultural barriers that have discouraged women and girls from seeking equal opportunities in all aspects of their lives. Since the Conference, the World Bank has almost doubled its lending to basic education, from about $500 million in 1990 to $1 billion in 1993. Similarly, UNDP doubled its expenditure and the United Nations Children's Fund (UNICEF) agreed to allocate one fourth of its total budget for basic education.

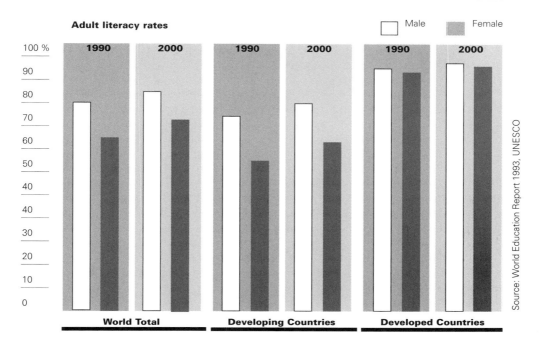

Adult literacy rates

☐ Male   ▨ Female

(Chart showing adult literacy rates with y-axis from 0 to 100%, grouped by World Total, Developing Countries, and Developed Countries, each for 1990 and 2000, with Male and Female bars.)

World Total   Developing Countries   Developed Countries

Source: World Education Report 1993, UNESCO

Why educate women?

There is a growing consensus now that education, irrespective of who receives it, contributes to development. It raises income, promotes health and increases productivity. There is also a consensus that when women are the recipients, the benefits are even more apparent.

Here are some reasons why:

- Better health: An educated mother can raise a healthier family. She not only knows about nutrition but also knows how to act during health-related emergencies. A mother's education may be more important to her children's health than flush toilets or piped water, or even food intake, says a UN Population Fund (UNFPA) report. It puts the difference in child mortality (deaths of children between one and five) as high as 9 per cent for every year the mother was at school. In Ghana, for instance, 52 per cent of uneducated women believed that illness was caused by spirits, but only 31 per cent of women who had been to primary school held this belief. In Peru, educated women were found to have healthier children regardless of whether a clinic or hospital was nearby. Another study shows that a one per cent rise in women's literacy has three times the effect of a one per cent rise in the number of doctors.

- Smaller families: Educated women tend to have fewer children, slowing population growth. According to a 1993 report of the Population Action Council, average family size and child death rates are lowest in countries such as Sri Lanka and South Korea, which combine strong family planning and health programmes with high levels of education for women. Conversely, they are highest in countries such as Ethiopia and

73

Malawi, where the level of female education is low and family-planning and health programmes are weak. In Brazil, uneducated mothers have an average of 6.5 children each, but those with secondary education have only 2.5.

- Greater productivity: Educated women are more productive both at home and in the workplace. A World Bank study of 200 countries showed that nations that had invested heavily in female primary education benefited through higher economic productivity. In Bangladesh, for example, women, who account for almost 90 per cent of the labour force in the garments sector, were found to be able to increase productivity and improve quality when given training. The World Bank concludes that failure to raise women's education to a par with men's exacts a high development cost—in lost opportunities to raise productivity and income and improve the quality of life. And at the family level, as women gain access to better employment due to better education, families benefit through higher earnings.

- Improved status: Educated women tend to make more independent decisions and stand up for themselves. According to a UNFPA report, in Kerala, India, educated women, however poor, seem to believe they have a right to good health care. But in Uttar Pradesh, also in India, illiterate mothers would not take their sick children to doctors without first obtaining permission from their husbands or in-laws.

- Social effect: Women, when educated, tend to encourage their children to become educated.

Educating women: Overcoming obstacles

If everyone agrees that educating women is such a good idea, why haven't we made more progress?

One reason is economic. Education costs money even when free schooling is available. First, there are school supplies to be bought and clothes to be made. More importantly, when daughters go to school, there are opportunity costs of lost work they could have done at home or in the market-place. World Bank studies show that in Nepal and Java (Indonesia), most young girls spend at least a third more hours per day working at home and in the market-place than boys of the same age.

Equally important are social and cultural factors. In many traditional societies, family and community attitudes are still hostile to female literacy. "Women who talk back to men stay unmarried", commented an African male at a recent UNICEF/non-governmental organization (NGO) conference. Often, husbands don't want their wives to attend literacy classes if they themselves are illiterate. "They get cross when supper is late", said a South African woman. Parents may want to send their daughters only to schools with female teachers, but in most low-income countries, only one third of primary, less than one fourth of secondary, and just over one tenth of tertiary education teachers are women. In some developing countries, parents may also feel it is unsafe to send their daughters to attend distant schools.

74

Problems for adult women are far more complex. Their work often begins before dawn and ends long after sunset. Describing the obstacles, UNESCO, in a recent report, painted this scenario:

Women in many developing countries are engaged for twelve to eighteen hours a day, every day of the week, in order to ensure the survival and well-being of their families. They must prepare meals and care for children, walk miles to find and carry back firewood and still more miles to get water. In certain parts of the world, women play the main role in growing food as well as in selling or trading it for other needed items.

Under these circumstances, how will it be possible for women to attend literacy or other classes, even if their husbands allow them to do so? And while they are in class, who will attend to their children?

The right to read

Education is a fundamental right. An equitable society, a goal set by the countries of the world in the Universal Declaration of Human Rights adopted in 1948, cannot be achieved if fundamental rights continue to be denied to half the world's population. "Gender apartheid is an obscenity", said UNICEF's former Executive Director, James P. Grant. "It won't end without educating girls."

A change in male attitudes towards women may help to improve the status of women. UNESCO feels that in terms of education there is at least one sign of optimism: more men are becoming literate. Since literate parents tend to send their daughters to school, the higher the literacy rate among men, the higher the literacy rate will be among women. Specific measures taken by Governments and NGOs have also helped close the gender gap.

- In India, the Government offers incentives such as midday meals and free education for girls up to grade seven. The Government has also launched a publicity campaign to eliminate gender bias in textbooks.

- In Zimbabwe, the Government has adopted a "policy of positive discrimination" in favour of girls. For years it practised a system of selecting an equal number of boys and girls for the country's sixth form. In the first years of the programme standards were lower for girls and it was difficult to fill the female quota. As a 1992 UNICEF-sponsored conference was told, they are now equal in both numbers and ability. Results show the sixth form as the only one where the male and female enrolment approaches equal numbers.

- In Ghorka, Nepal, Save the Children, an international NGO, encourages women to work in small learning groups. They meet in simple shelters, identify their own teachers, develop their own sense of group solidarity and organize men to do the construction. Over a two-month period, six nights a week, they receive basic literacy lessons. This is followed by a post-literacy system of women's production groups which include cash earning projects, such as fruit growing, local crafts and tree nurseries.

- In Burkina Faso, the Government reached more than 13,000 rural women by introducing boarding centres. Using ten national languages, the Government provided boarding centres during four residential sessions of 12 days each, spaced out with weekly breaks so the participants could return home to their families. This gave women a break from competing demands and duties at home.

The challenges ahead

The Fourth World Conference on Women in Beijing has suggested practical measures Governments can take to advance the status of women. In a draft Platform for Action, the United Nations Commission on the Status of Women identified four broad targets for advancing women's education:

- Ensuring women's access to quality education and training: A substantial quantitative and qualitative improvement of the education of girls and women needs to be made to achieve equality. Gender disparities should be forcefully addressed and gender-sensitive education and training should be developed.

- Achieving education for all: Top priority should be given to removing gender disparities from national policies and programmes for universal primary, secondary and higher education and adult literacy. More resources should be allocated to achieve equality in enrolment and prevent drop-out of girls from formal schooling.

- Preparing women for the twenty-first century: Measures should be taken to encourage women and girls to enter new fields of study, including science and technology. Lifelong training for women should be promoted, as well as women's participation in decision-making levels in education.

- Make education gender-sensitive: Action should focus on the elimination of social stereotypes from curricula, textbooks and training materials. Legal literacy components and information on human rights should be incorporated in the curricula. NGOs should play a more active role.

The dream still lives

Describing her dream of an ideal society, Christine de Pisan, a French courtier, wrote in the fifteenth century that since both women and men were equally intelligent, they should receive the same education.

Today, more than 500 years later, de Pisan's ideal has not been realized, but the dream remains alive. As the world prepares to enter a new millennium, the challenge it faces is to translate that dream into reality. The world has an opportunity to renew its pledge to equality and chart out a new course of action to further empower half its population. One key to their empowerment will be education.

When a woman is educated

The link between literacy and women's social status is undeniable. According to the documents of the World Summit for Social Development, held in Copenhagen in March 1995, education decisively determines a woman's access to paid employment, her earning capacity, her overall well-being and contributions to her family and to the society.

The Declaration and Programme of Action of the Social Summit make a strong case for educating women as part of the solution to the Summit core issues: poverty, unemployment and social disintegration.

A basic premise of the Programme of Action is that unequal access to resources, technology and knowledge has created unequal growth and led to increasing socio-economic inequality, both within and among nations. "Universal and equitable access to basic education for all children, young people and adults, in particular for girls and women, is a fundamental priority", the Programme of Action states. Ensuring equal opportunity is vital to a sense of human security. And human security, in turn, is crucial to safeguarding stability and peace in our world, it points out.

The inspiration for the Copenhagen Summit grew out of the General Assembly's determination, in the 50th anniversary year of the United Nations, to reaffirm the United Nations Charter goal of promoting "social progress and better standards of life in larger freedom".

By eradicating illiteracy and educating women, the world may get closer to that goal.

Two women

In Konkoran, a remote village in Mali near the edge of the Sahara desert, life has stood still for centuries. The only thing that moved was the water in the Niger River, which lately has been carrying diseases, parasites and the risk of river blindness. Thirty per cent of the children in Konkoran may die before the age of five, often due to water-borne diseases. Clean, safe water can save many lives. Several United Nations agencies have launched a literacy programme as part of a campaign about safe drinking water.

Like most other Konkoran women, Fanta raised animals to feed the family and provide income. She was one of the first to join the literacy programme. In addition to basic skills, like reading and arithmetic, Fanta learned about oral rehydration, or "life water", as it is called here. She now treats children with diarrhoea. Each week Fanta administers the dispensation of chloroquin to protect children from malaria. Fanta has also learned better methods for raising goats and healthier ways to prepare the milk—both for her family and for sale in the market. Village women who cannot read often come to her to write letters for them, or to seek advice on practical matters. "I never say 'no'," Fanta says with an amiable smile. Literacy has given Fanta's life a whole new meaning and a new level of status in her village.

A world away, in far-off Bangkok, Thailand, lives Youphadee. Her family is among the 400 who live in the sprawling Rajataphan slum, where she makes her living by selling food in the street. After Youphadee joined a literacy programme sponsored by the Government and UNESCO, she learned basic accounting. "I now can calculate what I need to run my business", Youphadee says proudly.

Besides learning to read and write, Youphadee also learned about hygiene and better ways to keep her home clean and dry. But like other women in the programme, she needed more than classes. Through their initiative, a day-care centre was added to the programme. She no longer has to worry about her children's safety while she and her husband are working.

Together with other women, Youphadee has also formed a credit union, which provides much-needed loans for family emergencies and investment in businesses. Youphadee is convinced education for girls is very important. "Educate girls because they have a more difficult life. If I had to choose between sending a boy or a girl to school I would send the girl", she says.

For both Fanta and Youphadee, literacy has been their passport to freedom. It has given them new confidence in their capabilities and enabled them to shape and control their own lives.

PORTRAITS OF HOPE

The four stories told here illustrate the realities of women's lives and their strength and capacity to overcome obstacles when they have the right advice and assistance. The stories also show the need for a women's development agenda that can create new strategies for promoting sustainable livelihoods and stable communities.

Gaining new hope in Rajasthan, India

Andu and her two daughters struggled to harvest a few bushels of wheat from their plot of land in the village of Nichlaphala in north-west Rajasthan. When city-based aid workers arrived in 1982 to suggest that villagers put half their land into mulberry trees to feed worms, Andu, along with everyone else, was suspicious.

Worms, the workers promised, would make silk, and silk would make money, more than enough to make up for the wheat. One village agreed to try it only after a project officer swore in front of statues of their deities that he would truly try to help them each step of the way.

Andu joined 300 women in 12 area villages and began to grow mulberry trees. The project of the United Nations Development Fund for Women (UNIFEM) in cooperation with the United Nations Development Programme (UNDP) provided silkworms and trained the women in sericulture: caring for the worms for the 25 days until they made cocoons, handling the cocoons, reeling off the silk and processing it into thread.

The women now take the cocoons to a reeling centre in the village of Sisarma, where they make the thread for sale to weavers all over Rajasthan. Andu makes about US$700 a year, nearly 40 times more than the average family income in India. She has earned enough to pay off her debts and has sent her daughters to a district college. "And I no longer have to work long, back-breaking hours in the fields", she said.

Her family's diet is much better, too. A mulberry tree's deep roots seek out underground water so that it can survive drought without irrigation. As it holds moisture in the soil, vegetables can be planted among the trees: cabbage, spinach, mushrooms, carrots—the first Andu had ever seen. She raises chickens on the scraps.

The project also set up community-based health education projects to help the villagers deal with broader problems. Once a month, women meet to schedule work programmes: distributing silkworms, making bamboo implements, supervising health centres and the local primary schools. They also have begun discussing social issues, such as how to combat widespread problems of promiscuity.

Another 1,100 families joined the sericulture programme in later phases that involved the World Food Programme and the UN Population Fund, as well as local agencies. But aid workers are slowly withdrawing now, as the villagers learn to run the operation themselves. Soon they will be independent entrepreneurs. Andu views her future with hope, saying "I am leading the kind of life that my mother could only dream of."

Confronting violence in Barbados

Her friends thought Elaine Hewitt was strong and courageous. In fact, the Anglo-Indian woman was being beaten regularly by her lawyer husband. "I thought if I kept quiet, by some miracle everything would become normal again." It didn't. The beatings went on for five years.

Globally, gender-based violence is generally ignored and sometimes even defended as a man's right. But at the 1993 World Conference on Human Rights, abuse of women was declared to be a violation of human rights.

"My daughter died in 1975 of cancer at the age of 15", Hewitt said. "After that, my marriage fell apart." Hewitt, a trained nurse who had moved to Barbados from England when she married, turned to Roman Catholicism. Her husband, coping with grief in his own, classic way, began to drink, and to beat her. "I never told anybody", she said.

Finally, 40 years old, penniless, helped by a few close friends, Hewitt walked out. She divorced her abusive husband and, with her two remaining children, forged a new life. Now she works for a small women's crisis centre and hot-line service in Barbados, speaking out about domestic violence through groups there and elsewhere that have come into existence to combat the problem.

"Before, everybody blamed the victim", she said. Judges and police asked what the woman had done to provoke her attacker. Everyone tried to ignore the situation. "Only in one case in 25 does the violence stop and the marriage recover", she said. "It is an enormous problem."

Hewitt became such an effective advocate that UNIFEM helped to bring her and other women to tell their stories at the Human Rights Conference in Vienna. Their testimonies were key to introducing the issue of violence against women and the concept of "women's rights as human rights". Policy makers finally acknowledged the existence of gender violence and incorporated that recognition into the document produced in Vienna. "Women don't have the luxury of only speaking of civil and political liberties",

Hewitt said there. "We don't have the luxury of only concerning ourselves with economic development issues. We don't have the luxury of compartmentalizing human rights. Women's rights to equity, personal safety and integrity are as important as the economic rights to food, jobs and health."

Hewitt refuses to cast blame. "We say the time has to come for people to get together and dialogue. Women must speak up, and men must speak up and ask for help to find out why they are behaving in this way. It isn't just women; the answer cannot lie with us alone. We need men to stand with us."

Now 55, Hewitt is proud of her achievements. She is also proud of her children, both college graduates. "My life is testimony that you can succeed no matter what", she said.

Learning skills for a better life in Cameroon

Mrs. Yebo Ruth, at 70 years of age, is the proud possessor of new skills and new income to help herself, her children and her grandchildren. Only a few years ago, she was one of many poor farming women in rural Pouma who could see that too much of the annual 10,000-ton harvest of cassava (manioc) was rotting before it could be used. Half of it went to make gari, a diet staple, but lack of fast transport to the city markets doomed the rest of the crop, even though the Government wanted to cut food imports.

Women produce an estimated 80 per cent of Africa's food. Yet some African Governments give more attention and support to the production of cash crops intended for export (tended chiefly by men) than they do to crops produced for domestic use (tended chiefly by women). Decisions concerning transport, currency controls, fuel and import policy are generally made by men, but greatly affect women by altering their market choices. When women's needs are ignored, however, everyone suffers. Sustainable development requires that the domestic food and food export sectors be linked in everyone's mind, and that policy makers recognize women's key role in national food security.

A private group called AID Cameroon looked at the problem of the cassava crop. They first offered to set up a project to buy bread made from cassava, for resale at the University of Cameroon. Mrs. Ruth was an eager participant. Then AID Cameroon with assistance from UNIFEM set up a cassava processing plant to produce gari, to be managed and owned by the 800 participating women. Mrs. Ruth quickly volunteered to be among those trained at a UNIFEM sister project in Ghana to learn how to run the project from sowing to market.

In Ghana, Mrs. Ruth learned techniques from picking cassava to heat-drying, from product packaging to work discipline and shift scheduling. AID Cameroon helped introduce better cassava varieties and developed distribution channels. Then a new problem arose; what to do with the mountain of peelings the new plant would generate?

Mrs. Ruth, along with the 32 women's groups involved in Pouma, learned to use the cassava peelings as fuel for the new plant's dryers, and thus increased gari's shelf-life. More peels are sold to local livestock breeders for fodder, and the rest go to the women's compost piles.

Mrs. Ruth's new income from the gari plant changed her life. She has been able to expand her diet to include fish and meat. She invests money in a savings plan that will eventually give her women's group ownership of the new plant.

Mrs. Ruth invests most of her funds in education for her grandchildren, particularly her granddaughters, whose school fees and medical bills she pays when their parents cannot. "They will have everything I can give them", she said. "They will learn for a better life."

Singing with a stronger voice in Brazil

"I began singing rap in order to say some things about what it was like to be a woman", said Cristina Batista, 22, lead singer and songwriter of a rap group called Lady Happy. "In singing we can give concrete examples of everything, understand what is happening to us." Cristina is the second-oldest daughter of a cook with five other children, none of whom know their father. She began singing for money at the age of seven and dropped out of school after the second grade.

In the hilly, impoverished fringes of São Paulo, young people confront enormous challenges as they grow up. In 1992, with UNIFEM support, the Black Women's Institute (GBWI) of Brazil set up Rap Bands, a self-help project for low-income young people. Rap Bands' weekly meetings offer music education and technical training along with information on Black history, gender issues and reproductive health.

"The Black woman is discriminated against twice", said disc jockey and rap singer Quettry, age 20, another project participant. "Once for being a woman and once for being Black. Therefore, our style is really political."

The young people integrate their concerns into rap songs. Twelve participating bands have already made many songs into hits by taking the music into clubs and dance parties and onto radio and television performances. The project reaches an estimated 5,000 young people every month.

"Lady Happy has two records out with two other groups", Batista said. "In the future I hope to make a solo record. Of course I will keep working on the project. It made things clearer for me."

Written in association with UNIFEM.

CHALLENGES AND OPPORTUNITIES

AFRICAN WOMEN: THEN AND NOW

By *Ama Ata Aidoo*

First there was Bob Geldof's Band Aid, which was staged in 1987 to raise both the international community's awareness of the plight of and funds for Ethiopia's drought victims. Then as recently as 1992, there was the more enduring picture of U.S. marines landing amphibiously and all eager to go feed Somalia's starving population. No doubt, both these events were extremely well-intentioned. However, there is also no doubt they helped to confirm a specific image of African women in the minds of the world. She was breeding too many children she could not take care of and whom she should not expect other people to pick up the tab for. She was hungry, and so were her children. In fact, it had become an idiom of photo-journalism for the U.S. and other Western visual media that the African woman looked old beyond her years, she was half-naked, her drooped and withered breasts were well-exposed, flies buzzed around the faces of her children, and she had a permanent begging bowl in her hand. Then just as people thought they had had enough of staring at Africa's shame, in 1994 they were given Rwanda and more recently, Burundi.

This is a sorry pass the daughters of the continent have come to. Especially when it is considered that we are descended from some of the bravest, most independent and most innovative women this world has ever known. We speak of The Lady Tiya of Nubia (ca. 1415-1340 B.C.), the wife of Amunhotep III and the mother of Akhenaton and Tutankhamen, who is credited with, among other achievements, leading the women of her court to discover make-up and other beauty-enhancing processes. Her daughter-in-law was, of course, the incomparable Nefertiti, a veritable black beauty whose complexion was nowhere near the alabaster she is now wilfully painted with.

Again from the Pharaonic era, we evoke Cleopatra: (69?-30 B.C.), about whom "more nonsense has been written ... than about any African queen mainly because of many writers' desire to paint her white. She was not a white queen. She was not a Greek," says John Henrik Clark with the impatience of painstaking scholarship in the face of half-baked ideas, prejudice and laziness. According to C.W. King, of Julius Caesar, Mark Antony and Cleopatra, the latter was "... the most captivating, the most learned, and the most witty." Among the many languages she spoke fluently were "Greek, Egyptian, Latin, Ethiopian and Syrian." Yet the great William Shakespeare, heralding contemporary Western racism, could only dismiss Cleopatra as a "strumpet", a whore.

Modern Africa came into collision with Europe towards the end of the 15th century, when prominent European explorers set out to "discover" the rest of the world. Two of these voyages proved significant for Africa. One was the journey of Vasco da Gama travelling from Portugal southward to find Asia. He passed the Cape of Good Hope in 1496. The other was, of course, Christopher Columbus's first voyage to the Americas. Legend has it that he stopped in the country soon to be known as the Gold Coast, now Ghana. There he built the ground compass, still visible near the beach on that bit of the Guinea coast, which the Portuguese later decided to name El Mina (as in "The Mine"!). What is absolutely certain is that since then Africa has never known peace. Soon came the slave trade, the ending of which was literally celebrated with the complete conquest and formal colonization of Africa in the middle of the 19th century.

No one teaches African history properly in schools or colleges anywhere, and that includes schools and colleges in Africa! Otherwise it would be common knowledge that in response to Europe's insistence on conquering the continent, Africa produced, over five centuries, countless women soldiers and military strategists, many of whom died in the struggles. One of these women was Nzingha (1582-1663), who tried to prevent the Portuguese from overrunning her country (Angola). She showed them what she was made of. On their part, the Portuguese demonstrated that they had not come to Africa on a mission of chivalry. They fought Nzingha with uncompromising ferocity and viciousness. When she suffered serious setbacks in 1645-1646, they captured her younger sister Fungi, beheaded her and threw her body into a river.

In fact, in pre-colonial times, fighting women were part of most African armies. For example, the all-female battalions of Dahomey (ancient Benin, early 19th century) sought to protect their entire empire against invaders and internal treachery. The Nzingha/Portuguese pattern was to be repeated in several areas of the continent over the next centuries. Queen after queen rose against the invaders. In the last years of the 19th and the early years of the 20th centuries, Yaa Asantewaa, an Asante (Ashanti, Ghana) queen, led an insurrection against the British. Although her armies were defeated, "it is safe to say that she helped to create part of the theoretical basis for the political emergence of modern Africa".

It could be granted that all these women were reigning monarchs who found it relatively easy to organize armies against foreign occupation. But then history is also replete with accounts of revolts led by women from non-monarchical traditions. An often-quoted example is the story of the women of Aba in Eastern Nigeria, who, in the 1920s, so successfully and collectively harassed the British that the colonial administration literally had to move headquarters, from Calabar to Lagos! Several years earlier in Rhodesia (Zimbabwe), Mbuya Nehanda (Nyakasikana) was accused of fomenting a rebellion against the British. In the end, the conquerors decided that the only way to get rid of their fear of this incredible woman was to hang her. And they did, in 1897.

In the years following the end of the Second World War, many women stayed in the forefront of the agitation for independence. In fact in revolutionary wars like the Mau Mau Rebellion of Kenya and the Algerian war of independence, we learn that the enemy often feared women guerrillas and guerrilla leaders more than their male counterparts. Today we know that the story of South Africa's fight against the institutionalized horrors of conquest would be different if women—including teenagers—had not been prepared to get actively involved. And they paid the price. They got killed, maimed, imprisoned and exiled. Better-known ones like Winnie Mandela, Albertina Sisulu and Zodwa Subukwe survived the hounding of men, only to later show an awesome readiness to carry the leadership torch with all the sacrifices such decisions inevitably entailed.

Given such a heroic tradition, it is a tragedy that the African woman today appears to be a weak victim, totally incapable of doing anything to help herself. If she has become such a creature, then we are convinced she is a mutant produced by the cumulative effect of the last five hundred years of relentless oppression, repression and suppression: first, through anti-female tendencies in our own indigenous societies, then by our conquerors and currently from a neo-colonial reality. These days, even our natural environments are behaving like implacable enemies!

From the early 1980s, life became especially harsh for the African woman, coping as she had to with the effects of the IMF/World Bank–imposed so-called structural adjustment programmes, so fashionable with our Governments then. They removed subsidies from her children's education, from health care, from food. In the meantime, transportation to and from vital areas of her life was also either broken down or had never existed. Added to all that was the fact that most areas of the continent were then gasping from severe droughts. So the world was phenomenally hot. The African woman had to give up on many seasons' crops, wondering quite often whether there would be enough water to last her and her children through the year for drinking, for cooking and to keep the body minimally clean.

Africa is the second largest continent in the world, covering a land area of over 30 million square kilometres. One or two other facts worth noting about the continent are that in spite of centuries of relentless exploitation by its conquerors, it is still, potentially, the richest piece of earth in the world. It has 60 per cent of all known exploitable natural resources. Furthermore, and in spite of the persistently vicious campaign about Africans and population explosion, Africa is not the most populous land on this earth. With all due respect, China is. In fact, given its size and its current population of around 700 million people, the continent is underpopulated.

To a certain extent, African women are some sort of a riddle. This is because, whether formally educated or not, "traditional" or "modern", we do not fit the accepted (Western) notion of us as mute beasts of burden. However, we are also not as free and as equal as African men (especially some formally educated ones) would have us believe. In fact, we fall somewhere between those two notions. To some West African men, the way West African women struggle to be independent "is really quite bad." They think that "these women are all over the place." Wherever and whenever men meet, you can be sure to hear numerous jokes and stories about women, all supposed to show how "terrible" we are. One solid "advice" any growing boy is likely to pick up anywhere along the coast of West Africa is: "Fear woman."

A few women have managed to squeeze some advantages out of the neo-colonial era, and have excelled in areas where women would not normally be expected to do so. The emphasis is on "few". Educational policies in Africa have never been democratic. They are mean, as in colonial times, or timid and lacking in confidence, as in now. Changes, where any, are at a snail's pace. Today, the pyramid is widely recognized as the symbol of what is happening to young women and girls in the educational systems of Africa: a massive base and a needle-point top. This is because, at the primary levels, girls and boys get equal opportunities to enter the system—or almost. However, as the years go by, the girls become fewer and fewer, until by the time a given age-group gets to the universities, the ratio of boys to girls is as high as 10 to 1, or more.

Apart from impossibly poor environments, this is due to the attritional effect of several negative forces on young women's lives. These include falling pregnant and getting expelled from school, while the offending males—whose identities no one cares to know—are left in peace to pursue their destinies. Or receiving discouraging career counselling from sexist teachers and other school authorities, schoolmates and sundry well-meaning but hopelessly reactionary relatives. Although when given the chance a number of young women not only show their independence and courage in choosing careers, but in most cases do brilliantly in them, women in high-powered positions in Africa, as elsewhere in the world, are still hostages to tokenism.

Indeed, one horrid fact that jumps out at anyone who tries to look for African women writers or women in any other high-profile professions is that they were always a batch of "onlys". For on our continent, millions of women and girl children were, have been and are being prevented from realizing their full potential as human beings, whether from the possibility of being writers and artists, doctors and other professionals, athletes or anything else outside the traditional roles assigned women. Of course, we know we share this and other symptoms of marginalization with women nearly everywhere. That is very cold comfort.

Whereas one is not saying that all the women in the world could be writers or dentists or architects if their basic needs for shelter, food, decent medical care and maximum education were met, it should still be possible to imagine how many hundreds more might be. Besides, if every single one of those millions of young women in Africa actually turned out to be a writer or some other professional person, wouldn't that be superb? (And that is quite conceivable with African women!) Yet we will never know how many of them have the potential because they never had even those limited opportunities which came the way of some of us. Consider this. In 1988, when I returned with my daughter to the United States after almost a decade, one factor that helped us settle was that we became part of an extended family network in the Boston area. There were six young Ghanaian women in this group who were then attending colleges in the area. Today, four are qualified physicians, one is doing her course work for a doctoral degree in French and the youngest should be graduating fairly soon with a Masters degree in Public Health.

For most African women, work is a reality, a responsibility and an obligation. They have drummed it into us from infancy. We could never have fought for "the right to work" —a major departure from a concern of early Western feminists. In West Africa, for example, virtually no family tolerates a woman who does not work. So today, there may not be too many homes in that sub-region, including traditionally Islamic areas, where growing girls would be encouraged to think they need not have ambitions because one day they would grow up to marry and be looked after by some man.

However, perhaps it is Africa's women farmers who get the worst deal of all. It may be fashionable now to admit that women are the backbone of the continent's agriculture. This is a recent trend. Earlier on, the existence of women farmers was not even acknowledged. Governments never mentioned them in agricultural policies. They did not appear in bilateral or multilateral discussions. So to the burden of constant poverty, of working on the farm from sunup to sundown and then coming home to take on dozens of other roles, was added the special deprivation of being invisible to policy makers.

All this should be enough to make African women want to fold their arms, keel over and just die. Yet we are doing anything but that. In spite of our problems, we are still pushing and struggling to be worthy heiresses to our past, to be planners today and builders of a better tomorrow. As anyone who cares for such comparisons might discover, in so many areas of human achievement, we can hold our own wherever women gather.

We need to intensify our struggle, though. Bisi Adeleye-Fayemi has added her voice to the call "to challenge layers of gender and class oppression, imperialism and exploitation" and seek "access to policy-making positions, legal reforms, equal rights in education, employment and credit facilities." Especially education. Because in our hands lies, perhaps, the last possible hope for ourselves—and everyone else on the continent. After all, we are one of the world's least touched resources.

Ama Ata Aidoo, a former Minister of Education in her native Ghana, is a novelist, playwright and poet. Currently she is teaching in the African and Afro-American Studies Department at Brandeis University, Massachusetts.

GRASS-ROOTS WOMEN'S MOVEMENTS GROW FROM CONFERENCE TO CONFERENCE

by Anita Anand

Sultana, a peasant woman from the northern valley of Gilgit in Pakistan, left her village for the first time to make a trip to the outskirts of Lahore. Her mission was to attend a meeting of peasant women organized by the Aurat Foundation and sponsored by the United Nations Fund for Women (UNIFEM).

Almost 100 women gathered under a large tent, speaking five different languages, sharing their life experiences. They discussed problems and possible solutions and met with politicians and policy makers. Many, like Sultana, had spent their entire lives in villages. Initially, they looked lost. But within a day they were sitting contentedly on a raised platform and talking comfortably into microphones, as if they had been born to public speaking. A women from Sindh said, "We have lived with these problems all our lives. Who can talk of them better than us?"

This meeting, in 1991, was not the first of its kind. UNIFEM had organized similar gatherings in India, Nepal and Bangladesh, with the idea that rural women should assist in designing national conservation strategies. Nigar Ahmed of the Aurat Foundation (Women's Foundation) said, "Our intention was to take the concerns of rural women to the legislators and policy-making bodies." And they have had increasing success over the last few years in all regions of the world.

Similar forums are bringing to public attention the issues and processes close to women's lives. A unique cross-fertilization is taking place between grass-roots women in urban and rural areas and women's organizations representing these interests at the local, state, national, regional and international levels. The range of women's non-governmental organizations (NGOs) and their mandate is wide. They are found in the North and South, in cities and villages, at the grass-roots and intermediary levels. They vary in form, style, goals, strategies. Yet, they all have a common denominator—they want to make the world a better place, starting with women.

Their history can be traced to the 1960s and 1970s, which were important years in shaping the UN Decade for Women (1976-1985). Several forces converged across continents: the struggles of the nations newly independent from colonization in Asia, Africa and Latin America; the civil, student and anti-war movements in Europe and North America; and fledgling women's movements in many parts of the world. Despite the fact that women had actively participated in the various struggles, they were still regarded as second-class citizens and not considered leaders.

Concurrent to the first UN conference on women in 1975 (the World Conference of the International Women's Year) in Mexico City was a gathering of NGOs, called the International Women's Year Tribune. For the first time in UN history, women came together to discuss how women from the grass roots could play an integral role in the social, political and economic planning of societies.

Mexico City was a landmark for women. It was here that women's lives, dreams and experiences were discussed, debated and shared. Sessions varied from the formal to informal, with film shows, exhibits and handicraft fairs. An information and documentation centre provided opportunities for participants to exchange views and information. Networking, by now a fundamental precept of the international women's movement, had its genesis here. The NGO Tribune took no formal decisions on the issues that were discussed, nor did it adopt formal resolutions or recommendations. But by 1980 women had become more deliberate and more strategic.

Almost 8,000 women descended on Copenhagen, Denmark for the mid-Decade Conference, the World Conference of the UN Decade for Women: Equality, Development and Peace. Women used whatever means they could to get to the NGO Forum. A Women's Feature Service reporter, Jill Severn, said, "One woman sold her car to buy a plane ticket. One used her annual vacation. And many others went into debt." The Copenhagen Forum attracted 2,000 more women than Mexico City. And while some sharp differences emerged between women from the South and North, equally important commonalities were discovered, which led to more sophisticated networking.

A few of the rallying points were violence against women, prostitution, women and development and the economic recognition of women's work. The emerging networks for these issues formed an impressive presence at the Forum '85, the parallel event to the World Conference to Review and Appraise the Achievements of the UN Decade for Women, held in Nairobi, Kenya. Fifteen thousand women attended and ran 125 workshops a day, a Peace Tent, a Film Forum, visits to rural projects, exhibitions and cultural events. NGOs had come a long way in magnitude and breadth since the 1975 Tribune.

When the Nairobi Forward-looking Strategies for the Advancement of Women to the Year 2000 (NFLS) were adopted in 1985, women's movements had much to celebrate. Their contribution to making valuable changes in the lives of women and society was starting to be recognized. The Nairobi conference suggested that national machineries —Governments and ministries—ought to create infrastructures that would enable women to move forward. These infrastructures would need to internalize at every level the mainstreaming of women into national development strategies. And women's NGOs were considered the fulcrum of the recommendations of the NFLS. Since 1985, women and NGOs have turned their strengths into a viable political force.

Women's Feature Service, an international news agency run by women and working exclusively with women journalists, itself grew out of the Decade for Women. Its network has grown parallel to the international women's movement's network. Women's Feature Service's mandate is to both develop women professionals and portray women's initiatives for change for the mass media. In this way the ideas, experiences and dreams of women can enter the mainstream. While the articles generally emerge from a situation of crisis—environment, water, sanitation, food security, civil war, conflict, disappeared sons and husbands, refugees, illiteracy and health—their purpose is to chronicle the long-term process of change of women in development.

Women's Feature Service has covered the same development issues brought up by recent UN conferences. On reproductive health, reporters in Latin America have generated a lot of material on abortion, since it is a major preoccupation of the women's movement there. Even in 1995, predominantly Catholic governments and legal systems still refuse to make safe abortions available to women. Women in Latin America and other regions are also concerned about primary health and reproductive health services, from menstruation to menopause. There has been a growing divide between overzealous population planners and women who feel their real-life reproductive health concerns have been ignored.

In January 1993, 19 women's health advocates representing women from Africa, Asia, Latin America, the Caribbean, the U.S. and Western Europe met to discuss how women's voices might best be heard before and after the International Conference on Population and Development (ICPD) scheduled for September 1994, in Cairo, Egypt. The NGO leaders initiated a "Women's Declaration on Population Policies", and a Women's Voices '94 Alliance to promote it. They asked the International Women's Health Coalition (IWHC), a U.S.-based organization, to serve as the Secretariat. The Declaration, modified and finalized by over 100 women's organizations in 23 countries, asserted that sexual and reproductive health rights were fundamental to all people. It spelled out a set of operating principles and programme strategies to ensure that these rights would be exercised, and called on national Governments and international agencies to reshape their policies to ensure health rights. The initiative, in content and process, was path-breaking in that the women's movement had never had such unanimity on the issues. For years, men and male-dominated organizations, of the North and South, had determined population policy. Then, for the first time, around the ICPD, women assumed center stage in the debate.

Alongside reproductive health issues, violations of women's human rights has been a motivating issue for women's NGOs. From almost all parts of the world—Asia, the Pacific, Western Asia, Africa, Latin America, Eastern and Western Europe and North America—came reports of violence against women. Women's Feature Service journalists wrote stories about rape, physical and mental humiliation, wife battering, incest, sexual harassment, kidnapping and genital mutilation.

After years of organizing—from discussions behind closed doors, to women-only forums, to national and international calls for action—at the 1993 UN World Conference on Human Rights (WCHR), the global community acknowledged that women's rights were being violated and that gender-specific human rights violations, as a distinct issue, were worthy of policy attention.

This came as a result of a worldwide petition drive calling on the UN to address comprehensively violations of women's human rights. More than 250,000 signatures from 121 countries in 21 languages were submitted to the UN Secretary-General. The campaign highlighted the importance of organizing at all levels—international, regional, national and local.

At the conclusion of the peasant women's meeting in Pakistan, Mumtaz Rizamani, president of the Sindhani Tehrik (Sindh Women's Movement) said, "The worst part of women's oppression is that we accept it as natural. But we have the power to change it. The Government will not do it for us, nor will funding from far-off places. We women should rely on ourselves and no one else."

As women's organizations have grown and matured, however, there is a recognition that Governments and funding agencies do have a role. They can facilitate or obstruct. As women began articulating their needs and problems in the home and community, the policy makers remained strangely silent. They did little to enact and enforce new legislation and policies. A major challenge for women became the prioritization of issues and strategies, and forging alliances across lines—North and South, rich and poor, rural and urban, grass-roots and elite, NGOs and Governments.

International grass-roots campaigns have put women's concerns on the international agenda through notable events tied to major UN conferences: The Women's Congress for a Healthy Planet (prior to the 1992 UN Conference on Environment and Development); the Women's Tribunal on Crimes Against Women (during the World Conference on Human Rights); Women's Voices '94 (prior to and during the International Conference on Population and Development); and the 180 Days/180 Ways campaign kicked off at the World Summit for Social Development on International Women's Day, 1995. Without the work of regional and national women's networks, the face of international environmental, human rights and population policy would be different.

In these UN conferences, women's alliances have attempted to insert a gender perspective and examine the socialization that defines women and men. Information on the experiences of women at the grass-roots level, who suffer the most indignities in society, is more readily available. Information has been gathered, analysed and presented to government delegations as they deliberate on the issues. These articulations are not academic and do not exist in a vacuum, but have been thought through by women and organizations with a commitment to change.

Women have argued, for example, that wife beating is not a personal matter between a man and woman, and rape is not an acceptable act of passion. They have pointed out that the inequity in wages between women and men in all professions, the lack of women in decision-making and political office and the absence of women in bilateral and multilateral decision-making are all responsible for and indicators of women being kept down. And while women's reproductive choices can shape their lives, women have not been adequately involved in reproductive health discussions and decisions. Decisions based on consensus are often tedious and time-consuming, but essential. The past lack of women's involvement has resulted in planning and strategies that have not worked.

Ideologies shape world views. The women's movement has called for the re-examination of predominantly male-dominated ideologies. Women have also grappled with the issues of politics and power—issues they have not been comfortable with, and with which they have little first-hand experience. For many women, the views which discriminate against women are unacceptable. But in the process of changing hearts and minds, dialogue rather than dismissal has been found to be more effective. Between the pressure imposed by women's organizations and the sensitivity of international and national bureaucrats, adoption of the progressive language at the ICPD was possible.

Sincere in the articulation of their concerns, women of grass-roots organizations use simple language. Issues of food security, livelihoods, health and the future of their children are primary. In organizing for Beijing, poor women in rural and urban areas express their most urgent concern: Why are we poor?

While designing the development decades, the international community and the United Nations have attempted to eradicate poverty. Some have argued that the present development paradigms have displaced people and aggravated poverty. Some have further argued that policy makers are so out of touch with the reality of the poor and disenfranchised, they cannot make or enforce policies to help them. Peasant women such as Sultana are well aware of their own problems. But the solutions are harder to devise.

The life experience of grass-roots women and their interaction with women who work as intermediaries is making it possible to bridge this gap. Policy makers—when lobbied by grass-roots advocates—have to listen because even the poor are their constituents. If equity is not an issue for policy makers, perhaps the voting power of women, at least in democracies, could convince them otherwise.

In many countries there is a mass mobilization of women to participate more actively in the political process. In 1993 the Indian Parliament passed the Panchayat Raj Bill, which established a 30 per cent quota for women as leaders in all district, block and village councils. Women's organizations took this opportunity to begin organizing on a mass scale. News reports from other parts of the world indicate that more women are entering politics in a strategic way.

The organizing in the last decade since Nairobi has shown that concerns of grassroots women have been put front and centre on the international agenda. Women are making history in revolutionary ways.

The goals of women's movements can best be realized when village women can be heard and taken seriously in the Governments, and when what happens in the Governments can be heard and addressed in the villages.

Anita Anand, from India, is Director of Women's Feature Service.

WHY WIDOWHOOD MATTERS

By *Martha Alter Chen*

"We are considered bad omens. We are excluded from all 'auspicious' events. We are expected to stay by ourselves. We are not treated as human beings with life, a body and emotions."

"I never worked outside our home before my husband's death. Now, my two unmarried daughters and I work as agricultural labourers. If I work too hard, I suffer chest pain and shortness of breath."

"I had to raise my children on my own. There was no one else to help me."

"When I was married, I was Mrs. Donnell. I was somebody. Now that my husband is dead, I am nobody!"

Widows are everywhere but they are rarely seen, let alone their concerns adequately addressed by public policy makers. Growing evidence of their vulnerability, both socio-economic and psychological, as evident from the feelings cited above, now challenge many conventional views about this "invisible group".

Almost everywhere around the world, widows comprise a significant proportion of all women, ranging from 7 per cent to 16 per cent of adult women. Yet, until recently, lack of data concerning widows contributed to the persistence of certain misconceptions about the prevalence and condition of widowhood.

For the first time, the misconceptions about widowhood are being challenged by the international community. Two prevailing myths, in particular, have been called into question. The first is that widows are elderly women whose children are fully grown. The second is that widows can rely on extended family networks for financial and emotional support.

Incidence of widowhood

The proportion of widows within countries or regions varies with fertility levels, mortality rates, differences in age at marriage and patterns of remarriage. However, the following patterns, presented in *The World's Women 1995: Trends and Statistics*, are discernible:

Overall widowhood: Among all adult women (15 years or older), the proportion of widows is highest in the developed countries, where greater longevity and low fertility rates increase the ratio of old to young people.

Older widowhood: Among women 60 and older, widowhood is significant everywhere, from 40 per cent in the developed countries and Latin America to 50 per cent in Africa and Asia.

Younger widowhood: In Asia and Africa, widowhood affects many women at younger ages. In many countries in these regions up to 20-25 per cent of women aged 45-59 are widowed, and in some countries up to 5 per cent of even younger women, aged 25-44, are widows. Looked at another way, the proportion of all widows who are below 60 years of age is 15.8 per cent in the developed world but ranges from 34.4 per cent (in Latin America) to 43.6 per cent (in Africa) in the developing world.

In brief, in developed countries widowhood is experienced primarily by elderly women, while in developing countries it frequently affects younger women, many of them while still rearing young children.

Whereas the incidence of widows differs across regions the incidence of widowers is uniformly low across all regions. Among adult men in all regions, the proportion of widowers is about 2-3 per cent. Thus the ratio of widows to widowers is high everywhere (averaging 4 to 1) generally due to men's older age at marriage, shorter life expectancy and higher rates of remarriage. Further, the consequences of losing one's spouse are different for men and women. In most societies, a widower not only has greater freedom to remarry than his female counterpart, but also has more extensive property rights, wider opportunities for remunerative employment and a more authoritative claim on economic support from his children. Had the living conditions of widowers been as precarious as those of widows, it is likely that widowed persons would have attracted far more attention.

Rules of widowhood

What happens to the woman whose husband dies? What are the duties and rights of widows in various regions and social groups? What if widows come from social groups which do not allow women to seek gainful employment outside the home? What if widows are forced to leave their husband's home or are forced off their husband's land? What if widows do not have children or have only young children? Where are they allowed to live? Can they remarry? Whom can they turn to for support?

Although social rules differ widely across cultures, most cultures have rules governing a woman's life. These rules have particular consequences for widows, especially in the absence of social support.

Across the different regions of the developing world, the degree to which women's lives are conditioned and constrained by local social rules are markedly similar. Most cultures restrict women in the following domains:

Residence: Most marriage and kinship systems dictate where a husband and wife should reside upon marriage. By extension, the rules of post-marital residence affect where a widow should reside after the death of her husband.

Inheritance: Most inheritance systems are patrilineal, restricting women's right to property. Even in countries where modern law affords women more equal rights to property, many social groups still follow traditional customary laws.

Remarriage: Most marriage and kinship systems have rules about whether widows may remarry and, if so, with whom. Some systems dictate that the widow should marry a brother of the deceased husband (usually a younger unmarried brother).

Employment: Across most developing countries, women face restrictions on employment opportunities, relating primarily to the gender division of labour. Aside from these general restrictions, widows face specific difficulties in seeking gainful employment. These include: lack of independent access to productive resources; weak bargaining power *vis-à-vis* men in economic transactions; frequent absences of a literate member in the household; limited access to institutional credit; and the burden of domestic work.

Social identity: Most marriage and kinship systems dictate specific, often stringent, rules to control the dress and behaviour of widows. Here are some examples of how such restrictions affect widows:

- In Asia and Africa, in some societies, a widow's in-laws may acquire control over her property by 'managing' it for her or by obtaining guardianship of her children. Or a widow, upon remarriage, relinquishes her own and her children's rights to her deceased husband's property.

- In South Asia, some social groups do not allow a woman to work outside the home even if her husband is absent or dead. In these social groups, a widow is expected to live only for her husband's memory, accepting the most austere of lifestyles.

A recent study of 562 widows in India shows that under the customary Hindu laws practised there, property rights for widows are widely acknowledged. However, these rights are often violated in practice. When a widow tries to manage the land on her own, without adult sons, her brothers-in-law often insist on share-cropping or managing her land themselves, or simply attempt to deprive her of her rightful share of the land. They try to legitimize their claim by arguing that they spent money on her husband's death ceremony or on her children's maintenance. In their attempt to gain control of her land, the brothers-in-law of a widow may go so far as forcing her to leave the village, or even—in extreme cases—arranging her murder.

Conditions of widowhood

The common restrictions on residence, ownership, remarriage and employment place widows in a situation of acute dependence on economic support from others. The extent and nature of family and community support becomes critical to their well-being (and the well-being of their children). Despite social ideals of support and protection, widows in many regions of the world are the most economically, socially and physically vulnerable group of women within given populations. This suggests that social ideals may not be reflected in practice.

Without data concerning financial transfers between family members, it is impossible to measure directly the extent to which widows receive or are denied support from family members.

Data on household headship and economic activity among widows, particularly those under 60, are more readily available and are suggestive of the support widows receive. Among all women aged 15 to 59, widows are the most likely to head their own households, even when compared to separated and divorced women. By contrast, the proportion of male householders who are married far outnumbers those who are widowed.

In developing countries, the levels of economic activity among widows aged 15 to 59 is higher on average than among married women. Whereas in some societies these elevated levels of economic participation may reflect the greater freedom afforded single women, in other societies these levels of economic participation reflect the need to generate household income despite restrictions on women (both married and single).

However, where widows are relatively older than non-widowed women, the activity rates of widows may be lower. A recent study in Egypt found that widowed women in Egyptian society are relatively older and have a higher illiteracy rate than non-widowed women. Moreover, only 16 per cent of the widows were currently working or involved in income-generating activities. And yet 88 per cent were living separately from their parents or in-laws.

Since the poorest segment of a population is usually comprised of female-headed households, households headed by widows probably face greater economic hardships than most. Regrettably, for most countries, the lack of income data disaggregated by headship and marital status prevents the direct documentation of the economic vulnerability of widow-headed households, suggesting the need for greater attention to this area in future surveys.

However, several recent studies from South Asia document the economic and mortality risks of widows. A study in Bangladesh found a much greater decline in the economic status of widows compared with widowers. Women's access to resources was found to be much more dependent on marital status and living arrangement than is the case for men. Another study of widows in India found that households headed by widows had, over a period of 15 to 20 years, sold or mortgaged a disproportionate share of their land. Several studies also found that households with a widow have lower per-capita expenditure levels than households without a widow.

Economic deprivation is likely to be reflected in high morbidity and mortality rates among widows, compared with married women in the same age group. A study on the impact of widowhood on mortality among Bangladeshi women aged 45 and above found that widows tend to have much higher mortality rates than married women in the same age groups. The mortality rates for widows can be quite different depending on their living arrangements: widows living alone emerge as the highest-mortality group; widows who head households with an adult son present emerge as the lowest-mortality group. A study in India found that for women above 45 years of age, the mortality rates are 86 per cent higher among widows than among married women.

102

Proportion of women (ages 15-59) who head households

	Total	Married	Separated/ Divorced	Widowed
Developed	14	4	76	85
Africa	9	6	41	86
Latin America and the Caribbean	9	6	57	68
Asia	6	4	38	55

Source: Neiv Duffy, 1994. Background note for the second issue of *The World's Women 1995: Trends and Statistics* (United Nations publication, New York)

Why widowhood matters

Growing evidence from around the world suggests several reasons why widowhood matters as a social problem in the developing world.

* *Many more women than men face the likelihood of being widowed for a significant portion of their lives.*

* *Many women are widowed when they are young and remain widowed the rest of their lives.*

* *Most widows face customary rules restricting their options regarding residence, inheritance, employment and social interactions.*

* *Many widows cannot depend on support from their in-laws, parents, brothers or even daughters.*

* *Given that adult sons are the most reliable source of family support, young widows are economically and socially more vulnerable on average than older widows.*

Around the world, older widows have received most of the attention (if any) that has been paid to widows, whether in studies of ageing or under State-run pension schemes. However, given that adult children (particularly sons) are the most reliable source of support for widows, it is childless widows and widows with minor children who are at special risk. And, on average, younger widows are more likely than older widows to be childless or to have minor children.

The growing evidence on widowhood argues for a full review of the legal, policy and cultural practices contributing to the special deprivations of widows, particularly where widows are likely to have dependent children. Widows clearly experience special difficulties and deprivations connected with the restrictions imposed on their lifestyles and the persistence of negative social attitudes toward them. Given that the social ideals of support and protection for widows are less widely reflected in practice than the social rules restricting widows, it is important to pay attention to widowhood as a particular cause of deprivation and to undertake public action and policies in support of widows.

103

Four areas of public action and policies stand out as being critically important to widows:

1. Securing and protecting widows' rights to property;

2. Promoting employment and economic opportunities for widows;

3. Designing and implementing special social security schemes for widows who cannot work; and,

4. Undertaking social reforms to create a more positive social identity for widows.

One final point: There is something quite astonishing about the fact that the needs of millions of widows around the developing world have been so consistently neglected in more than four decades of planned economic development. The reasons for this neglect would be worth probing.

One of them, evidently, is the fact that the deprivations of widows are so well hidden in economic and social statistics as they are commonly reported. The standard household-level economic variables, in particular, tell us little about the well-being of widows as individuals. Moreover, household-level economic variables disaggregated by headship but not by marital status tell us little about the well-being of widow-headed households compared with other female-headed households or with male-headed households.

Another reason is the fact that the living conditions of widows in developed countries is not as precarious as those of widows in developing countries. A related reason is the fact that, within developing countries, the living conditions of widowers are not as precarious as those of widows. Had the living conditions of widows in developed countries and of widowers in developing countries been as precarious as those of widows in developing countries, it is likely that widowed persons would have attracted far more attention from the international community.

A third, critical reason is the prevailing myth surrounding widowhood in developing countries, namely, that widows are protected and cared for by extended family networks. So long as this myth persists, widowhood will be treated as a family matter, not as an issue for public policy. Had the often precarious living conditions of widows in developing countries been more widely studied and known, widows would have attracted far more attention from the international community.

Dr. Martha Alter Chen is director of the programme on non-governmental organizations at the Harvard Institute of International Development (HIID) and a lecturer at the Kennedy School of Government at Harvard University.

REFUGEE WOMEN

The explosion of ethnic conflicts in the 1990s, as the end of the cold war unfroze long-dormant disputes, has created humanitarian crises whose number and magnitude seem to increase dramatically every year. In 1994, the scale and geographical spread of such violent upheavals reached proportions that have few parallels in recent history. In tiny Rwanda, in the space of less than four months, between half and two thirds of the country's population was killed, died from epidemic diseases, or fled. It was the largest and most catastrophic exodus the United Nations High Commissioner for Refugees (UNHCR) has ever witnessed. Among the hardest hit by the violence and uncertainty of displacement were young girls, elderly widows, single mothers—women.

Protection is at the heart of the responsibility the world bears towards refugees. Protection means freedom from assault. Deprived of the protection of their state, detached from their families and communities of origin and considered helpless foreigners in an alien land, refugees are, by definition, in any culture, vulnerable to violence. Refugee women and their children are the most vulnerable of all. Despite the strength and courage that has carried them out of their homelands, refugee women have special needs for shelter, supplies and health care. They also require measures to protect them from sexual violence and exploitation in all phases of their lives as refugees.

The problem is vast, though a complete picture is not available. Statistics on refugees and asylum seekers are, even today, rarely broken down by gender. UNHCR estimates that 23 million refugees and 26 million internally displaced people have been forced to leave their homes because of conflict, massive human rights abuse, or the direct effects of conflict, such as famine and lawlessness. As a rule of thumb, more than three quarters of those destitute displaced people are women and their dependent children. That proportion of women and children may rise to 90 per cent in some refugee populations, when husbands or fathers are killed, or taken prisoner, or drafted as combatants. Most take refuge in remote, poorly developed areas where there is little security. Many have already been attacked—exactly how many is simply not known. "Sexual violence against women is widespread", says UN High Commissioner for Refugees Sadako Ogata. She calls the phenomenon "a global outrage".

Sexual violence and exploitation

Rape is a common element in the pattern of persecution or terror or "ethnic cleansing" that drives refugee families from their homes and civilians increasingly become the intentioned targets—rather than the accidental victims—of warfare. From Myanmar to Somalia and Bosnia, refugee families frequently cite rape or the fear of rape as a key factor in their decision to leave.

Subsequently, the road to asylum is itself paved with threats of sexual violence and exploitation. The perpetrators may be bandits, smugglers, border guards, police, military and irregular forces on both sides of the border, or elements of local populations taking advantage of defenseless arriving refugees. The need to cross military lines or regions affected by lawlessness or civil war to reach safety puts women and girls at particular risk.

Once in exile, women and girls are still vulnerable to sexual violence or exploitation by camp officials or other refugees. Some countries automatically incarcerate people who enter without visas in detention centres, often alongside hardened criminals. Sometimes they detain women or young children together with adult men. The potential for abuse in such circumstances is obvious. In camps, refugee women may be forced into sex in exchange for material assistance for themselves or their children—particularly if the distribution of basic supplies is left to all-male camp committees. Officials, too, sometimes sexually coerce women in return for rations or identity papers. Domestic violence often escalates with the pressures, disruptions, confinement or enforced idleness of refugee life. Later, victims of sexual violence may be further assaulted because of the shame they are alleged to have brought on their society.

In 1993, the incidence of rape was reported to be alarmingly high at camps for Somali refugees in Kenya, which were located in isolated areas plagued by bandits and Somali militia. Hundreds of women refugees were raped in night raids, or while foraging for firewood. UNHCR set up a pilot project to improve protection. The camps were fenced with thorn-bushes and protected by expanded patrols. Vulnerable women were relocated to safer areas. Community outreach was expanded. Several victims of violence, who were suffering from acute forms of ostracism, were relocated to other refugee camps or given more rapid opportunities for resettlement abroad.

How to protect refugees from sexual violence

UNHCR has developed formal guidelines for preventing and responding to sexual violence, based on detailed recommendations by field workers experienced with the rape and piracy attacks on Vietnamese boat-people, the rapes of Somali women in Kenya, or the barbarous 'ethnic cleansing' rapes of Bosnian women. The guidelines aim to provide field workers with practical, non-specialist advice on the medical, psychological and legal ramifications of sexual violence. They are also intended to dispel the discomfort of many refugee workers with such acts—or any tendency to dismiss them as an inevitable by-product of social breakdown. Ann Howarth-Wiles, UNHCR's Senior

Coordinator for Refugee Women, calls the guidelines "a fundamental primer" that should "immeasurably improve the sensitivity and skills of people who work with refugees, whether for UNHCR or our implementing partners".

UNHCR has also developed gender training, known as People Oriented Planning (POP), to encourage staff to focus on the protection and assistance needs of refugee women. A key element is encouraging women to participate in camp decision-making and the distribution of basic supplies. When men claim that women have no traditional role in decision-making, UNHCR staff encourage women to form separate committees. The alternative—leaving key decisions and distribution in the hands of all-male groups—has in the past led to the theft or misuse of key supplies, sexual exploitation, and the failure to supply key basics to vulnerable families, especially those headed by women.

Not every group of refugees can easily accept the empowerment of women. The problem is compounded when refugees come from conservative societies, which may react to exposure to a foreign environment by even more extreme practices. UNHCR staff report that among Afghan refugees in Pakistan, the practice of purdah has actually intensified during exile. Women who had previously worked in fields alongside male members of their family are no longer permitted to even leave their compounds, because of the mixing of various tribes and communities in the camps. To ensure proper health care for these women, and a modicum of skills, literacy and nutrition training, UNHCR has taken steps to increase the number of its female staff officers—who must often focus their initial, confidence-building efforts on elderly women (less socially restricted) and young children.

In an emergency situation, a proper focus on women's particular needs may, in practice, be close to impossible to maintain. Faced with an overwhelming inflow, such as the quarter of a million panicked and dying people who daily flooded out of Rwanda in the first few days of August 1994, field staff can often do little more than identify a few members of the most vulnerable groups, and perhaps sketch the basic foundations of intelligent camp design. In emergency situations, refugee families may be obliged to share tents. Hastily constructed latrines and washing facilities may offer little privacy, or be located too far from living areas. In extreme circumstances, sufficient food may not be getting to the most vulnerable members of a social group, such as widows with children, or elderly women on their own. Such circumstances are not acceptable, and are never tolerated for long. UNHCR field staff are, without exception, committed to maintaining proper assistance to all refugees.

Redefining women's refugee status

Many women have trouble substantiating their claims to refugee status, especially if those claims are based on sexual persecution. Though no gender restriction was intended, the 1951 Convention Relating to the Status of Refugees that is the bedrock of UNHCR's work was written using male pronouns. It defines a refugee in terms of

Where are all the refugees?
Figures as of April 1995

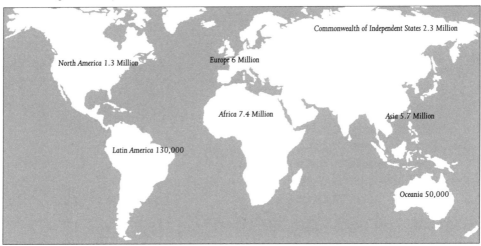

Source: UNHCR

a well-founded fear of persecution based on race, religion, nationality, political opinion or "membership of a particular social group". UNHCR has issued policy statements encouraging countries to consider that when rape or other forms of sexual violence are committed for reasons of race or political opinion, for example—and particularly when this is condoned by the authorities concerned—then it should be grounds for refugee status.

Some countries have recognized this, and in addition have ruled that women who face inhumane treatment because of perceived transgressions of social mores should be eligible for refugee status, as members of a "particular social group". Canada, for example, has recognized that a woman should be considered a refugee if she fears that she may be persecuted in her home country because of her refusal to inflict genital mutilation on her baby daughter, or to wear heavy, restrictive clothing. There has been similar progress on issues of gender-based persecution in Germany, the Netherlands and Switzerland. In 1984, the European Parliament determined that women facing cruel or inhuman treatment because they seemed to transgress social mores should be considered a particular social group for the purposes of determining refugee status. UNHCR has encouraged the Parliament's Member States (as well as all other countries) to formally adopt this interpretation.

Still, few countries employ women staff in their refugee status determination procedures, despite the quite obvious reluctance of most refugee women to discuss sexual persecution with men. Many States dismiss allegations of sexual violence as irrelevant to refugee status. Indeed, many countries rarely consider the asylum claim of a married woman separately from her husband. Only sustained and active lobbying byUNHCR and other refugee groups can hope to change this situation.

110

Preparing refugees for independent life

Most refugee's goal is, ultimately, to return home once conditions of peace and stability have been re-established. Women are no different—and of course should have their own say in fundamental decisions such as repatriation. Because refugee women are often single heads of households, with limited education or income-generating skills, well-designed and targeted development-oriented activities can be crucial to preparing them for independent lives when they return. These activities should not be seen primarily as an attempt to influence long-held cultural values. Usually they are a common-sense assessment of the traditional role held by women in that society—taking into account the role of women in agriculture, animal husbandry, or, more simply, the health and nutrition of their children. In April 1993, the social services specialist participating in an emergency team sent to Benin quickly recognized that destitute single mothers were being forced into prostitution to survive. Implementation of income-generating activities saved many from this fate.

Income-generating and skills-training activities in exile are often carried over to returnee communities, as part of UNHCR's small-scale Quick Impact Projects (QIPs) to boost infrastructure and development. In Nicaragua, "QIPFEMs" were designed specifically for returnee women, concentrating on non-traditional skills such as bee-keeping, agriculture and reforestation, and on the construction of hand-pumps, threshing mills and day-care centres to reduce women's domestic workload. Returnee women were also given loans so they could set up cooperatives and businesses. Contracts with UNHCR's implementing partners in Nicaragua commonly stipulated that women must benefit from at least 50 per cent of wage-earning, income-generating and training opportunities provided by QIPs, and they should receive equal pay. As a result, the income, skills, expectations and confidence of returnee women rose dramatically, and traditional communities became familiar with the concept of women as economic actors.

The Cairo International Conference on Population and Development in September 1994 recognized that "reproductive health care and family planning are vital human rights". Those vital rights are still absent from many refugee camps. UNHCR and UNFPA have embarked on a series of joint activities to promote reproductive health for as many refugees as possible. A practical guidance manual for reproductive health is being developed, based on the experience of dozens of field officers. The aim is to provide refugee health services with guidelines to deal with gynaecological diseases as well as with broken legs and cholera. Better health facilities will be able to treat complications resulting from the genital mutilation of baby girls and the resulting tearing during rape or marital sex. They will provide female examiners and counselling on nutritional advice, AIDS and sexually transmitted diseases, as well as access to family-planning information.

111

Sustaining a culture

Women are the life-sustaining force of any refugee community. Together with their dependent children, they often form the numerical majority of a refugee population. They also play a central economic and social role. They have the power to nurture future generations, re-establishing the family and culture in exile and re-creating it again on return to their homeland.

Although UNHCR has always intended that female refugees should receive equal, adequate and appropriate benefits, UNHCR activities have not always been planned with full regard to the needs, abilities and aspirations of refugee women. Neglect of their particular needs has at times meant that programmes, from health clinics to skills training, have benefited male refugees disproportionately. The result, in every case, has been an unnecessary and wasteful degree of dependency—weakening not only women but the community as a whole.

Action to raise the consciousness and power of refugee women can have incalculable and enduring benefits for an entire population. "In exile, we women became very united, of necessity, although we did not know each other", says Maria Eugenia, who returned to El Salvador in 1988 after many years of exile in Honduras. "We were 11,000 refugees all together, most of us women. It was up to us to organize and pro-mote our needs. We stated our problems and sought solutions in every area. We received training in areas like health and education and agriculture; people started to learn skills. We had chicken farms and different types of workshops, making clothes and shoes. When we returned, we had changed. Here, outside in the countryside, peasant women used to be ignored. We did not vote; we had no voice. Now, thanks to UNHCR, and to our organization while we were refugees, that has changed. We have a voice. We make it heard."

Written in association with the Office of the UN High Commissioner for Refugees (UNHCR).

EQUALIZING GENDER OPPORTUNITIES

By Mahbub ul Haq

In no society today do women enjoy the same opportunities as men. Despite much progress in the last two decades, gender disparities persist in many fields. There are two durable impressions from the record of the last two decades:

First, women have made considerable progress in the last 20 years in building their basic capabilities and in closing the gender gaps in education and health. Some of the evidence is quite powerful:

- *In adult literacy and combined primary and secondary school enrolment, the gender gap was more than halved between 1970 and 1990 in developing countries. The rising education levels for women were a fairly universal phenomenon during this period. The Arab States led this advance by more than doubling their female literacy rates.*

- *Also remarkable is the rapidly closing gap in higher education. In developing countries, female enrolment at the tertiary level was less than half the male rate in 1970, but by 1990 it had reached 70 per cent. In 32 countries, more women than men are now enrolled at the tertiary level.*

- *Female life expectancy has increased 20 per cent faster than male life expectancy over the past two decades. High fertility rates, which severely restrict the freedom of choice for women, have fallen by one third. Maternal mortality rates have been nearly halved.*

It is true that, despite such rapid progress, many gender gaps still persist in education and health and there is still a formidable agenda for progress in several countries. Of the total 900 million illiterates in the world, women outnumber men two to one. And maternal mortality rates continue to be, on average, 35 times higher in developing countries compared to industrialized countries—a totally unacceptable situation. But the last two decades have witnessed much progress and there is a reasonable chance of eliminating these gender gaps in education and health over the next decade or two through a determined effort.

Second, despite such improvement in women's capabilities, their participation in economic and political opportunities remains limited. The doors to the corridors of power are opening but opening slowly and reluctantly. Some telling examples:

- Of the 1.3 billion people in absolute poverty, about 70 per cent are women. Poverty still has a woman's face. [1]

- Despite a two-thirds increase in female literacy during the last two decades, their participation in the formal employment sector has increased by only 3 percentage points - from 37 per cent in 1970 to 40 per cent in 1990.

- The female wage rate is, on average, three fourths of the male wage rate because women are concentrated in the low-paid, non-formal sector, and often receive a lower wage for equal work.

- In many African countries, women account for more than 60 per cent of the agricultural labour force and contribute up to 80 per cent of total food production—yet receive less than 10 per cent of the credit to small farmers and 1 per cent of total credit to agriculture.

- Women still constitute less than one seventh of top administrators and managers in developing countries.

- Only 10 per cent of parliamentary seats and 6 per cent of cabinet positions are occupied by women today. Politics continues to be a male domain, despite women having half the vote.

- Women put in longer work hours than men in almost all countries that have been surveyed but most of their work remains unpaid, unrecognized and unvalued in national income accounts.

These, then, are the two contrasting trends in the last two decades: increasing female capabilities on the one side and restricted opportunities on the other. Such a wide gap between capabilities and opportunities leads to a considerable waste of women's potential and, naturally, to a rising level of frustration. The previous three UN women's conferences have greatly helped to raise the world's awareness about these issues and were instrumental in putting considerable pressure on Governments to accelerate their investment in the education and health of their women and in equalizing women's rights under the law. The main challenge for the Beijing Conference is to open the economic and political doors that are barely ajar.

Many of these issues are analysed at length in the forthcoming 1995 Human Development Report, commissioned by UNDP and due to be released in August 1995.[2] The report also suggests two composite indexes for measuring gender equality and ranking countries on a global scale, assesses the value and contribution of women's unpaid work and suggests a concrete strategy for equalizing gender opportunities. The report argues convincingly that human development, if not engendered, is endangered.

The Beijing Conference needs a concrete plan of action. It is, of course, for the Member States of the United Nations to chart out such a programme. But let me offer some proposals for the consideration of the global community, totally in a personal capacity. First, all Governments must agree at Beijing to eliminate the remaining gender gaps in education and health over the next decade (1995-2005) through an accelerated investment in providing basic social services to women in every country. The main focus of this effort must be in the developing countries since the industrialized

114

countries have already achieved near-gender equality in education and health. The total bill for such an effort is estimated at around $20 billion a year. This is roughly 5 per cent of the total size of public sector budgets in developing countries today. Most of this additional effort can be financed from restructuring existing budget priorities—particularly through some judicious cuts in military spending, reduction in the losses of inefficient parastatals (through privatization) and elimination of inappropriate development projects. The Copenhagen World Summit for Social Development has already endorsed the 20:20 compact to provide basic social services to all the people over the next decade and recommended it on a voluntary basis to interested and willing developing countries and to their donors. It is essential that this compact be made gender-sensitive. In expanding the coverage of basic social services to all people, women should be given priority because of their past neglect. *All nations should agree in Beijing that they will make sufficient investment in the next decade to eliminate the gender gap in basic human capabilities.*

Secondly, special institutions must be set up to provide credit facilities to poor women and to empower them to enter the market. Lack of access to credit—as well as to other productive assets, particularly land—is often responsible for denial of economic opportunities to women. Women are regarded as uncreditworthy with no collateral to offer. Formal credit institutions do not bank on poor women. Normally, less than 10 per cent of bank credit is allocated to women. Some countries are beginning to design innovative credit institutions, on the pattern of the pioneering effort made by the Grameen Bank of Bangladesh, to provide credit to poor women for setting up micro-enterprises or other service activities for self-employment. But these national efforts remain modest. And there is no international institution giving serious and sustained support to these national programmes. *The Beijing Conference should recommend that a special window be set up as an "International Grameen Bank" in one of the existing multilateral institutions to help developing countries launch their own national credit institutions for poor women.* A beginning is being made at present in the World Bank; this is a useful start and the global community can build on it.

Thirdly, one of the most important challenges for the Beijing Conference is to *set a time-table—say, the next ten years—over which all nations should pledge to extend equal legal rights to women.* It is now 16 years since the United Nations approved the Convention for the Elimination of All Forms of Discrimination Against Women. Yet as many as 90 countries have either not signed the Convention, or signed without ratification, or ratified with reservations. The first order of business is to bring the moral pressure of the global community on these reluctant nations to accept the basic tenets of legal equality. It is also necessary to organize transparency of information and worldwide projection of some outrageous instances of legal inequality. This is one of the tasks that should be assumed by a UN Agency for the Advancement of Women, proposed later.

115

One aspect of violence against women has not been covered in international law. In several countries, in conflict situations, violence has been directed against women as a weapon of war, particularly by the organs of State—witness the rape of helpless women in Bosnia. Such violence should be declared a war crime, punishable by an international tribunal. This is a rising concern in the present international situation that the Beijing Conference must address.

Fourthly, it is quite clear that the free workings of the economic and political processes are unlikely to deliver equality of opportunity because of the prevailing inequities in power structures. When such structural barriers exist, government intervention is necessary—both through comprehensive policy reforms and through a series of affirmative actions.

The recent experience of the Nordic countries is a fitting response to those who question the effectiveness of affirmative action. Within the last two decades, the Nordic nations of Denmark, Finland, Iceland, Norway and Sweden have moved fast to achieve near-equality between the sexes through several affirmative actions: quotas for women in political parties; representation in cabinets; paternity leaves to supplement maternity leaves; less working hours for young parents; and many thoughtful changes in social security systems.

The Beijing Conference must issue a forceful call for affirmative actions by participating nations since the normal workings of the existing economic and political processes will never deliver gender equality.

Fifth, the Beijing Conference must move fast to remove a yawning institutional gap. The world needs a high-powered UN Agency for the Advancement of Women (UNAAW).[3] Such an Agency will keep the women's concerns on top of the global agenda on a regular basis so that we do not have to wait for women's conferences every decade to remind the international community about this forgotten issue.

There is a great deal of confusion and controversy about the proposal for such a woman's agency. Those UN agencies which are already in the field but are rather small, with limited mandates and even more limited resources, worry that they will be further marginalized. Others argue that women's concerns are all-embracing and cannot be pigeon-holed in a separate agency: all agencies should deal with them. These vested interests can only hurt women's concerns.

A distinct agency, like UNAAW, can become the most ardent and professional advocate for gender equality and for monitoring progress on international and national commitments. Such an agency would neither replace nor take away from existing WID programmes or from existing UN agencies. It would only lend them further strength by filling a policy vacuum on this issue at the global level.

116

Still an unequal world

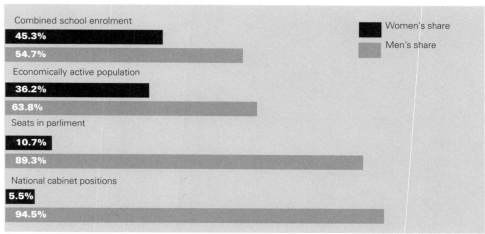

Source: 1995 Human Development Report, UNDP

These are only a few concrete proposals. Much more is needed. Gender equality is not a limited technocratic issue. It is a wholesale political process. It touches all areas of social, economic and political life. The relentless struggle for gender equality will go on far beyond the Beijing Conference. But the Conference must mark a departure from the past by initiating a number of concrete steps. Too much has already been said about gender equality. There is a time when eloquence must give way to action.

Dr. Mahbub ul Haq is the former Finance and Planning Minister of Pakistan and currently Special Adviser to UNDP Administrator and the main architect of the annual Human Development Reports. *This article represents only his personal views.*

1. Khadija Haq, "Poverty Has a Woman's Face", Our Planet, volume 7, number 2, 1995.

2. UNDP, Human Development Report 1995, Oxford University Press.

3. See the proposal made by Khadija Haq in "Gender Priorities for the 21st Century", published in United Nations and the Bretton Woods Institutions, Macmillan, April 1995.

ACTION

MOVING BEYOND RHETORIC

By *Gertrude Mongella*

"A revolution has begun and there is no going back. There will be no unravelling of commitments—not today's commitments, not last year's commitments, and not the last decade's commitments. This revolution is too just, too important, and too long overdue."

These were my words to representatives of Governments and non-governmental organizations who attended the 39th session of the Commission on the Status of Women (CSW), the final preparatory committee meeting for the Fourth World Conference on Women. After three weeks of intensive and detailed negotiations, they had reached agreement on the draft Platform for Action, the main document for discussion and negotiation by Governments at Beijing. The text still contained bracketed phrases, signifying the need for further compromise on language. But clearly, one thing would not be compromised—the principle of equality between women and men.

The aim of the Beijing Conference is to capitalize on the strength and resourcefulness of women, to share it and to act on it. The Conference is not about business as usual; it is about changing the status quo. We must all recognize once and for all that women are not guests on this planet; rather, we represent about 50 per cent of the world's population, and we demand our rightful place in our societies. Change must come about because change is right, and because improvement in our status is essential if we are to move the world towards a better life for all individuals—men, women and children—in all nations.

The preparations for this historic Conference have demonstrated that there is a strong international consensus for action. The Platform identifies 12 critical areas of concern and recommends more than 200 specific actions to be undertaken by Governments, the international community, the private sector and non-governmental organizations to address them. We must apply concrete solutions to the obstacles and constraints that women continue to experience in the political, economic, social and cultural spheres.

Recent United Nations conferences on the environment, human rights, population and social development have repeatedly articulated the pivotal role and needs of women; for example:

- When Governments addressed the question of environmental degradation at the UN Conference on Environment and Development at Rio de Janeiro in 1992, they recognized that policies would fail if women were not involved;

- At the World Conference on Human Rights at Vienna in 1993, Governments declared that the rights of girls and women were "inalienable, integral and indivisible" from other human rights, and transcended nationality and culture;

- At the International Conference on Population and Development at Cairo in 1994, Governments affirmed women's right to reproductive health, including availability of a range of safe, effective methods of family planning and the means of solving reproductive health problems; and

- Governments agreed at the World Summit for Social Development at Copenhagen earlier this year that development could not be achieved nor poverty eradicated without investment in women.

These United Nations conferences have shown that what have been called "women's issues" are finally being recognized as issues of importance throughout society. Nations now see that it is imperative to address the "gender dimension" in finding solutions to a whole range of problems that face today's world.

The preparatory process for the Beijing Conference has been as inclusive as possible, embracing Governments, the United Nations system, national committees and non-governmental organizations. Five regional planning meetings involving all these bodies have been held, and each has produced, by consensus, its own platform for action. These documents have brought each region's perspective to light and, seen together, they also demonstrate a strong commonality of needs and concerns.

We have been saying all along that women and men must work together if we are to bring this world safely and successfully into the coming century; so, too, must we have the participation of young people. In one of its most exciting projects, the Secretariat for the Beijing Conference launched an innovative programme that integrated youth into the preparatory process. Each regional meeting included a forum for young people, and a number of their recommendations were included in the regional platforms.

The UN also sponsored Expert Group Meetings covering such key areas as education and training; women in decision-making; gender and the agenda for peace; and institutional and financial arrangements for implementing and monitoring the Platform for Action. The conclusions reached by these Expert Groups later received consideration by CSW in drafting the Platform.

In addition, non-governmental organizations in almost every country of the world mobilized, conducting forums, engaging in dialogue with Governments and contributing to shaping the regional and UN platforms. They gave a voice to countless women who otherwise would not have been heard.

The theme for Beijing is "Action for Equality, Development and Peace". These global issues have concerned Governments since the first world conference on women met at Mexico City in 1975. The Mexico City conference marked the beginning of the UN Decade for Women; it was followed by a mid-decade conference at Copenhagen in 1980 and an end-of-decade conference at Nairobi in 1985. At Nairobi, the "Forward-looking Strategies for the Advancement of Women to the Year 2000" were adopted. This document was to serve as a blueprint for improving the status of women and was a major advance towards integrating women into broad-based mainstream activities.

The Strategies have not yet brought women to where they need to be, and that is why commitment and action are the keys for Beijing. Enormous challenges still face women in 1995. Over one billion people in the world today live in unacceptable conditions of poverty; the great majority of these are women, mostly living in developing countries. More than two thirds of the world's 900 million illiterate adults are women, and according to UNESCO, at least 60 million girls are without access to primary school education.

Five hundred thousand women die every year—one every minute—of pregnancy-related causes, most of which could be prevented with basic, comprehensive reproductive health care, including family planning services. Twenty million women suffer from complications of pregnancy and childbirth; these figures could be reduced through adequate nutrition and access to appropriate health services, as well as through men sharing responsibility for sexual and reproductive behaviour.

Exploitation of and violence against women and girls is a continuing reality throughout the world. Girl-children are sold into prostitution, and some of the richest countries cannot promise women a safe street to walk on—or even a safe home. Women also suffer disproportionately from escalating civil and ethnic conflict; 80 per cent of the world's almost 50 million refugees and displaced persons are women and children.

During the last two decades, increasing numbers of women have entered the labour force in both industrialized and developing countries. Forty-one per cent of the world's women aged fifteen and over are economically active. But the increase in women's employment has not been accompanied by improvement in occupational status, security or income. The majority of women, particularly rural women, continue to live as "hewers of wood and drawers of water" in a world characterized by science and technology. Women tend to be concentrated in traditionally "female" occupations—low-status, low-wage jobs, including part-time and night-shift work, with no societal or trade-union support. Worldwide, the percentage of women executives and managers remains very low. And women still earn, on average, only 50 to 80 per cent of the pay of their male colleagues.

In government, women continue to be poorly represented. In 1993, with the exception of the Scandinavian countries, women made up less than nine per cent of members of parliament throughout the world—a little less in fact, than in 1987.

What have we learned since Nairobi? There has been some progress, but not enough fundamental change. Women the world over have, in some ways, made great gains in society, securing recognition of their human rights and gaining access to education, health and social services. Almost universally, women have the right to vote, to hold office and to represent their countries in the international arena. Yet where it matters most—at the levels of decision-making in national and international policy—women, beyond a token number, are still excluded. This is unacceptable in a world that extols democracy.

The Platform aims to make Governments accountable to women, and that demands the re-examination of priorities and the reallocation of resources, as well as commitment to specific actions. It entails the enactment, review and enforcement of laws so as to afford women equal opportunity, development and physical safety. Accountability requires policies for involving and advancing women in political and economic decision-making. Governments must take the leading role in ensuring that institutional and financial arrangements are made to enable and motivate institutions to carry out the Platform's mandate.

Action must be taken within the United Nations system to enable it to mobilize nations toward global consensus on these issues. The agencies that focus on women's status need stronger structures and resources in order to facilitate women's advancement within Member States. Secretary-General Boutros Boutros-Ghali has called for "major changes in the management culture, the system of appraisal and accountability and the recruitment and promotion process" within the UN Secretariat, with an eye towards gender balance. In the UN as in the world at large, women's rights and potential are keys to solving the world's most serious problems.

As always, the involvement of non-governmental organizations is essential to progress. It is the NGO that most effectively reaches the individual girl or woman. Person to person, NGOs have immediate impact on problems. NGOs are the democratizing force in this process, the agents of change.

The private sector, ever more powerful, must also contribute to positive change, because it touches almost every aspect of women's lives and every area of critical concern in the Platform. Women need to be equal, active stakeholders and decision-makers in the private sector, just as they must be in the public sector. Beijing will be the first of the world conferences on women to bring the private sector into the dialogue and partnership for women's advancement.

The question of financial resources and arrangements must be addressed, and during the coming months, the Conference Secretariat will be clarifying the financial resources required to implement the Platform. The Platform indicates that Governments, despite their constrained resources, will need to commit themselves to further assistance. The prospect of realizing long-term fiscal and social gains will have

to drive a reallocation of resources away from wasteful, destructive military expenditure into investments in women. But if money is crucial, so too is political will. It takes will, not financial resources, to set a target or mandate for female parliamentary representation. Outlawing discrimination based on gender is free.

The Fourth World Conference on Women must elicit commitments to action, coupled with commitments of resources. This is the mission of Beijing: not further analysis, but meaningful action. Each Government must now set priorities, specify the resources it will contribute and declare what steps it will take to hold itself accountable to the world's women. It is time to move beyond rhetoric and work towards genuine change.

Gertrude Mongella, from Tanzania, is Secretary-General of the Fourth World Conference on Women (Beijing, 4-15 September 1995).